W
SC
SHOULD
RULE
SCOT
LAND
1997

WHY SCOTS SHOULD RULE SCOTLAND 1997

A CARNAPTIOUS HISTORY OF BRITAIN FROM ROMAN TIMES UNTIL NOW BY

ALASDAIR GRAY

CANONGATE

FIRST PUBLISHED
IN SCOTLAND, 1997, BY
CANONGATE BOOKS
14 HIGH STREET
EDINBURGH EH1 1TE

THE QUOTATION FROM
EUROTRASH IS FROM
IRVINE WELSH'S
THE ACID HOUSE
PUBLISHED BY JOHNATHAN
CAPE LTD, 1994.

ISBN 0 86241 671 X
*BRITISH LIBRARY
CATALOGUING-IN-
PUBLICATION DATA*
A CATALOGUE RECORD
FOR THIS BOOK IS
AVAILABLE UPON REQUEST
FROM THAT LIBRARY.

TYPESET BY PALIMPSEST
BOOK PRODUCTION
POLMONT, AND
PRINTED BY CALEDONIAN
INTERNATIONAL
BISHOPBRIGGS, SCOTLAND

TO
SCOTT
PEARSON
WITH
THANKS
FOR ALL
HIS HELP
WITH
THIS AND
MANY
OTHER
BOOKS

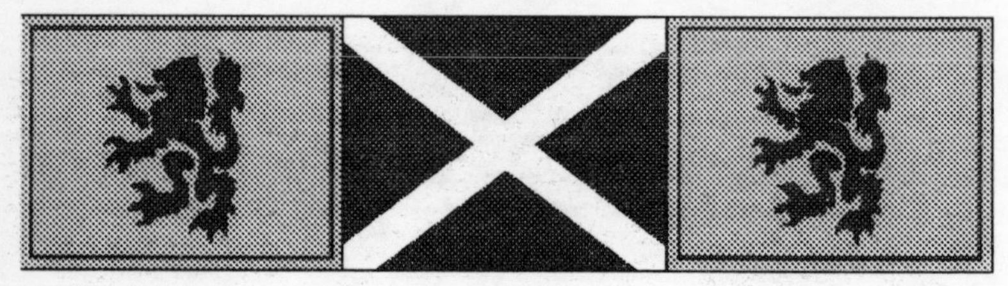

C O N T E N T S

INTRODUCTION

THE FIRST PAMPHLET with this name was written quickly for the British general election of 1992. It was my first polemical work and I was pleased with it; pleased also that reviewers treated it kindly.

With a view to reprinting I read it carefully three months ago and found it a muddle of unconnected historical details and personal anecdotes with a few lucid passages and at least one piece of nonsense – Chapter Four spoke of *The Protestant Scottish Conscience (or Soul)* as if it was a predictable thing many people had, though even influenza takes different forms in different bodies. The only excuse was that I had dictated the pamphlet aloud instead of writing by hand. The reviewers' kindness had been the condescension instinctively given to the art of children or half-wits.

The pamphlet you now read is therefore not a revised version of the first. It is completely rewritten, though it retains some of the old lucid passages. I have also kept the voice of my publisher, who asked down-to-earth questions when I lost myself in too many details or rhetorical flights. The year of publication is now part of the title because the last chapter fails to bring the book quite up to date, and any version printed after 1997 will be enlarged to make it that.

I also include a story based on bad dreams which came while brooding on the state of Scotland today. Good luck to critics who think the whole pamphlet is fiction. It may still provoke intelligent thought.

I like most of England. I say so because the 1992

pamphlet made one English reader (who otherwise liked my writing) ask why I hated it. He either believed that only hatred can explain a Scottish wish for home rule, or that my historical account of England showed scorn of it. But I nowhere condemn or praise whole nations, and am certainly not pleased with my own.

Some Scots hate England, of course. Their frame of mind is diagnosed by Irvine Welsh in a short story called "Eurotrash". The narrator meets a Dutchman who denounces Britain saying:

> *We Dutch went to Africa. You British oppressed us. You put us into concentration camps. It was you people who invented the concentration camp, not the Nazis. You taught them that, like you taught them genocide. You were far more effective at that with the Maoris in New Zealand than Hitler was with the Jews. I'm not condoning what the Boers are doing in South Africa. No way. Never. But you British put the hatred in their hearts, made them harsh. Oppression breeds oppression, not resolution.*

Says the narrator:

> *I felt a surge of anger rise in me. I was almost tempted to go into a spiel about how I was Scottish, not British, and that the Scots were the last oppressed colony of the British Empire. I don't really believe it, though; the Scots oppress themselves by their obsession with the English which breeds the negatives of hatred, fear, servility, contempt and dependency.*

That unhealthy state of mind will always occur while most Scottish opinion has no influence on how Scots are ruled. But it is not my state of mind.

1
THE GROUND OF ARGUMENT

READERS WHO LIVE in Scotland but were born elsewhere may feel threatened by the title of this pamphlet; I must therefor explain that by *Scots* I mean everyone in Scotland who is able to vote. This definition excludes a multitude who live and vote abroad yet are Scottish by birth or ancestry, yet includes many who feel thoroughly English yet manage Scottish farms, hotels, businesses, industries and national institutions. It includes second or third generation half-breeds like me whose parents or parents' parents were English, Irish, Chinese, Indian, Polish, Italian and Russian Jewish. It includes seventy-two members of parliament who mainly live and work in London and some absentee landlords who occasionally visit ancestral Scottish estates to shoot, hold family parties and vote. This book is aimed at all voters north of the Solway–Tweed boundary because, whether born here or recently arrived, it is they who should elect the government of Scotland. But they don't.

I argue that by being in Scotland you deserve a government as distinct from England as Portugal from Spain, Austria from Germany, Switzerland from the four nations surrounding her. My argument is not based on differences of race, religion or language but geology. Landscape is what defines the most lasting nations. The big rice-growing plain of eastern Asia explains why the Chinese nation is the largest, most peopled and most ancient. Another highly self-centred nation was made possible by successive layers of limestone, chalk and clay forming a saucer of land with Paris in the middle. The Baltic Sea explains why such close neighbours as Norway, Sweden and Denmark have different governments though similar languages and populations which, if united, would be less than two fifths of England's.

But no natural barrier can contain human curiosity, greed and desperation, so invasions and migrations have kept national boundaries expanding and contracting like concertinas. Roman geographers were first to map two big islands they called *Britannia*. They saw that, like Gaul, these were naturally divided into three parts which they named Albion, Caledonia, Hibernia. Albion was the south part of the biggest island: very woody and marshy yet offering few natural barriers to the march of the Roman legions. The tribes of Albion combined to repel the legions and were defeated. South Britain got planted over by Roman camps joined to each other by well-built roads and to *Londinium*, Britain's first capital city. The biggest camps were sited in the most fertile places and at the best places to bridge the rivers. They grew to be the centres of towns which thrive to this day: Bath, York, Lincoln, Carlisle and every city whose name ends in *chester* or *caster*. The geography which helped the Roman occupation explains why the English Catholic and Protestant Churches have been officially ruled from Canterbury since AD 596; why the English state has been ruled from London since 1066, and has two ancient universities in what were market towns near the capital.

The legions later marched into Caledonia. The Pictish tribes here also combined to repel them and were defeated, but Caledonia was hard to keep and expensive to administer. Firths, sea lochs, chains of high moorlands and mountains made north Britain like a cluster of big islands jammed together in the east and coming apart in the west. Soil which could be cultivated lay in districts cut off from each other. The natives, though defeated, had secure wildernesses from which to counterattack. As Edward Gibbon put it:

> *The native Caledonians preserved their wild independence for which they were not less indebted to their poverty than their valour. Their incursions were frequently repelled and chastised, but they were never subdued. The masters of the fairest and most wealthy climates of the globe, turned with contempt from gloomy hills assailed by the winter tempest, from lakes concealed in a blue mist, and from cold and lonely heaths, over which the deer of the forest were chased by naked barbarians.*

The geography which helped to repel Rome explains why the Scottish Church, Catholic and Protestant, had no locally based archbishop or single official to command it; why Scotland had no single capital city before James VI emigrated to London in 1605, but four ancient universities in very different cathedral towns.

Gibbon says the Romans calculated the number of legions and ships they would need to conquer Hibernia but decided conquest there would also be too much trouble. The only part of that island convenient to the British mainland was the north-east corner nearly touching Caledonia. This explains why the only part of Hibernia now belonging to mainland Britain is the north-east corner, despite seven centuries of trying to subdue the whole island by frequent doses of indiscriminate massacre. The strangest thing about Hibernia is that

Christianity took root here outside the Roman enslavement system and produced a highly literate monastic culture among small tribal kingdoms. The Hibernian tribes were called Scots in those days. Caledonia belonged to the Picts, though Norwegians sometimes occupied her northern and western shores.

It sometimes seems that every nation in Europe has had a spell of bossing others in defiance of natural boundaries, yet every empire is at last undone by the appetite for home rule and inability to rule ourselves well while bossing neighbours or foreigners. The Roman legions were returned to Italy in AD 404 because their slave-based empire was being attacked by nomadic tribes out of northern Asia. The Britons of Albion were almost immediately raided by Scots from the west, Picts from the north and German pirates from the east. Am I boring you?

PUBLISHER: (apologetically) The reader may be wondering how this ancient history helps the argument. You began by saying Scotland's geology – the lie of the land – made her a different nation.

AUTHOR: It does, but like every other European land a great mixture of folk has poured into this irregularly shaped national container, a mixture to which people still add themselves. I am partly writing to persuade incomers to think of themselves as Scots by explaining why earlier incomers came to think so. The force that pressed or stirred a mixture of races here into a self-governing nation was often trying to shake it apart. That force was so often English that I cannot start my argument without saying how the English came to south Britain and Scotland to the north.

PUBLISHER: But in this size of pamphlet the result will be a kind of children's history!

AUTHOR: I hear that nowadays many children and adults too have been taught little or nothing of history. It is adults I want to teach so here goes.

When the Romans left south Britain it was almost immediately raided by Scots from the west, Picts from the north and pirates from the east. The pirates were pagans from north Germany where they had farmed land in forest clearings, defended their crops with their swords and worshipped Thor and Woden. Pressure or example of the nomad invasions was moving them westward, so Britons invited them in to help expel the Picts and Scots. They expelled them so completely that in two centuries the natives of Albion had also been killed, enslaved or expelled into Cornwall, Wales and Strathclyde. These settlers eventually called themselves English, and the completeness of their conquest is astonishing if we recall that the folk they conquered were descended from builders of Stonehenge and tribes the Romans had not easily defeated. The explanation is that by finally submitting to the Romans (who historians consider a *civilizing* people despite their use of torture and massacre as public entertainments) the Britons grew too weak to preserve their own culture.

The English had little use for the Roman towns and military strongholds, thinking them causes of slavery. They lived in self-supporting farm communities ruled by councils of elders. When a warlord was needed for defence the elders joined neighbouring councils to elect a king. Kings were continually needed. As the settlers drained marshes and cleared forests the land attracted more Germans and Scandinavian invaders. Soon England contained six warlike pagan kingdoms with Northumbria one of the greatest. It spread up the east coast from the Humber, and the fewness of natural barriers made it possible for Northumbrians to occupy the most fertile part of Pictland up to the Firth of Forth. That is how the English language entered Caledonia.

While Britain was being Anglicized from the east some Scots sailed from the top right-hand corner of Hibernia and made a kingdom in the western islands and peninsula of Argyll. This new Scottish kingdom had Christian priests who read, wrote and built upon Iona the first British monastery outside Ireland. For five centuries Scottish, Irish and Norwegian kings were buried there. Priests trained in Iona brought Christianity to Picts in the east, Strathclyde Britons to the south, thus helping the Scots kingdom to spread through all these lands, though conquest, intermarriage, alliances against English and Scandinavian invaders also helped. In 846 a Scot ruled all Caledonia except the Northumberland part south of the Forth. Gaelic speakers called the Firth of Forth the English Sea because it separated them from Sassenachs.

It is good to know that language difference did not stop Scottish missionaries entering England and Christianizing it through Northumbria while the missionaries of Pope Gregory were doing that from Canterbury. The first vernacular poem in English literature, Caedmon's *Genesis*, was dictated in a Northumbrian monastery founded by Gaelic monks. Which proves that different cultures can combine creatively.

PUBLISHER: Fascinating, perhaps. Is it relevant?

AUTHOR: Yes, because I can now explain why the English north of the Tweed became Scottish. They were driven to it by an oppressive new government centred on London. This turned them into defenders of a frontier which again separated different governments though not different languages. These English helped to make Edinburgh a Scottish capital city.

PUBLISHER: Do you hope that the English who have recently settled in Scotland will help to do the same?

AUTHOR: Yes. Scotland needs all the help she can get, though London rule has not quite reduced her to the state of Britain under Rome.

2
FEUDAL & CLAN SYSTEMS

WILLIAM, BOSS OF NORMANDY, belonged to a fourth or fifth generation of Scandinavian pirates who had made themselves overlords of western Europe. He had a claim to the English crown which the English council of local leaders ignored. They elected Harold, one of their own nation who had been ruling England wisely and well as the previous king's minister. William decided to take the nation by force. He got the other Norman lords on his side by promising to double their French estates by the addition of estates across the channel. They believed him because at land grabbing he had already proved himself deadly efficient. In a Europe with a very primitive money market he borrowed enough to hire mercenary soldiers from French neighbours who would otherwise have attacked Normandy when he left it. Then he left it and added England to his other possessions.

The job was not easy. Though his soldiers were all professionals who lived by warfare the English were mostly farmers fighting for their land. For five years William fought uprisings in the south and east and west (where the English were helped by their old enemies, the Welsh) but resistance was strongest in the north. Here two other former enemies, Scots and Danes, helped the English. William paid the Danes to go away then burned homes, crops, farms and farming tools. His massacres drove English survivors into Scotland. Famine stopped them returning – shires north of York were deserted for half a century.

The north never bothered William again. After six and a half centuries south Britain was again owned by a military empire on both sides of the English Channel. Nearly all England's gentry were killed or exiled by William, so now he could give his poorest mercenary soldier land with a village or two on it, his barons estates of a hundred manors or more. On these they built great strongholds from which England was ruled for the next three centuries. It was now the most thoroughly feudal state in Europe, under the permanent martial law of fighting landlords whose commander conferred with them in the House of Lords. When not fighting the landlords liked to hunt.

England still had forests where the pigs of commoners could forage and the English catch deer or smaller game when poor crops reduced their diets. William was an excellent man-killer because he disliked most people, but he loved the deer he hunted and was merciless to others who did so. In Hampshire he fenced off a private hunting ground by clearing farms, villages and religious houses from between the woodlands and his landlords followed his example on a smaller scale. The English natives were excluded from a source of cheap meat by game laws threatening them with death, though seven centuries later this penalty was changed to transportation for life. In the nineteenth century Norman property laws were used to evict hundreds of Scottish communities from their land, and even nowadays the remaining natives can be arrested for taking a bird or fish from the land where they live.

Along with other natural rights the English were robbed of a language. Their original speech and splendid literature were gradually forgotten as the commoners improvised a new speech that made sense to their bosses. Meanwhile wealthier folk sent their children to schools where they learned Norman French, which had no great literature but gave them a chance of defending themselves in the conquerors' law courts.

PUBLISHER: You seem obsessed with the Norman Conquest.

AUTHOR: I am! It enrages me more than earlier robberies with violence because power-loving historians and teachers used it – perhaps still use it – to warp children's minds. They praised Roman invaders because they brought a kind of peace and spread Christianity. They praised English invaders because their way of choosing aldermen and kings was a kind of democracy. They could only praise the Normans for their efficient feudal system, so they romanticized it. The English were taught to be PROUD of having been conquered because – though painful at the time – it gave them a tougher class of managers who, centuries later, led them to thrash the French at Agincourt and seize the British empire.

PUBLISHER: Maybe it did.

AUTHOR: (*wildly*) Agincourt and the British empire were ALSO robberies with violence! Children should be taught it is WRONG to take riches from foreign lands by military force, COWARDLY to gun down spear-throwing natives, VICIOUS to mass bomb civilians and grounded soldiers in Kuwait and Iraq!

PUBLISHER: Calm down – you'll make some readers fling the book away. I admit Duke William was not a nice man but were Scottish kings better?

AUTHOR: No better. Malcolm Canmore, son of the Duncan killed by Macbeth, ruled Scotland from 1069 to 1093 and raided England five times, attempting in the north what William was doing in the south. He lacked troops to hold the land he invaded so could only keep looting it and retreating. When English kings counter-attacked Scotland he avoided battle by apologizing and swearing allegiance to them, then broke his promise. On his fifth raid he was trapped and killed. Compared with Duke William the Scottish king was a coward, liar and failure, but his power to hurt was limited by the number of people he ruled and by Scottish geology.

The population of eleventh-century Scotland was about 300,000 to England's 1,750,000. It had few towns and the peopled parts were isolated from each other by more or less mountainous wilderness. Even the plain between Forth and Clyde was divided between Gaels with Irish relations in the west, English with Northumbrian relatives in the east, so everywhere the social organization was in clans who could only fight clannishly. Clans were extended families where everyone had the surname of their chief who sometimes inherited the job from his mother's side of the family. As in African and north American tribes the agricultural work was often done by women while men hunted and fished. Hunting weapons are as efficient against people as against deer and wild cattle – one reason why Normans forbade hunting to the English. Clan chiefs showed their efficiency by leading raids upon their neighbours so Scotland, though not feudal, was often feuding. Regard Scotland as a cluster of small nations, each with good reason to fear its neighbours, each with a chief who supported the king because, with the king's help, no neighbour could finally conquer him. That was the clan system. Its essential difference from England was in the king's title – he was King of Scots, not King of Scot*land*. England's king was also a warlord but owned the whole land by right of conquest. He had given his barons counties in return for the oath of allegiance – their promise of military service. The counties were divided into estates of knights who held them in return for *their* oath of allegiance. That was feudalism. Neither system was perfect. Feuds were as chronic between Scots clans as civil wars between Anglo-Norman nobles.

PUBLISHER: Why describe these two systems? Modern readers will think them then equally nasty.

AUTHOR: Because the struggle between them turned this Scotland of squabbling chiefdoms into a new kind of European nation – one whose king only ruled because he had proved his fitness to the Scottish commoners – despite the fact that he was a greedy murderer who began by betraying the Scots to their enemies.

PUBLISHER: Oh dear. Am I about to hear the story of Bruce again?

AUTHOR: (firmly) The story of WALLACE and Bruce. All who write about Scotland come to it.

3
NATIONAL THEFT & RECOVERY

or,
John and William go to Westminster

WHEN FEUDAL INVADERS had subdued the native peasants they could only fight each other, so France had Europe's richest soil, poorest peasants, grandest nobility and endless warfare. In 1095 Pope Urban directed this belligerence into the first crusade. As French lords mustered their troops they were surprised to be joined by soldiers in outlandish armour. These were Scots who no lord had summoned or expected, because Scotland was still outside feudalism.

It was brought there thirty years later by David I, a Scots king who had helped Anglo-Norman barons in one of their civil wars. He saw how feudal law could be used to subdue unruly clans, so declared himself not just ruler but *owner* of Scotland, and in return for their oaths of allegiance, gave his chieftains title-deeds to their clan territories. This altered nothing until he invited in some Norman barons and gave them Scottish estates in return for *their* oath of allegiance. The estates were in fertile plains and valleys often raided by highlanders. These barons (Baliol, Bruce, Comyn and others) still owned English estates in return for their allegiance to the Sassenach king. English speech now spread steadily through the Scottish lowlands, though proximity and intermarriage made most Scots bilingual. The Scottish court had two poet laureates, one for each language. But no king could have held Scotland together without the Church.

Before the sixteenth century Scotland's population was about half a million – less in time of plague. There were no towns in the highlands and those in the lowlands were too small to support a secular middle class of the sort developing in England with nearly eight times as many people. The Scottish middle class was its clergy. They had religious houses throughout highlands and lowlands. Their preachers lent the king a broadcasting network that spoke to places his heralds could not reach. David I bought their support with larger grants of land than he gave his Anglo-Normans. The Church repaid him with two fifths of the royal revenue, for the abbeys farmed good land by the newest methods, growing more grain and wool than other communities. The earliest recorded coal mining and whisky distilling in Scotland was by monks of Dunfermline. The Church kept schools, hostels, hospitals and funds for relief of the poor. Only through the Church could the clever son of a labourer achieve the social power of a lord.

For nearly a century the nation thrived for a while under kings who kept peace by negotiation more than warfare, and by marrying the princesses of Scotland's potential enemies, English and Norwegian. Their courts moved in a yearly circuit between Edinburgh in the main approach to the English border, Stirling in the gateway to the highlands, Dunfermline north of the Forth. In 1286 Alexander III died leaving no heir and peaceful growth gradually stopped. *Thirteen* nobles claimed the throne but the claims of Baliol, Comyn, Bruce were strongest and equally so. A strong, impartial adjudicator was needed to prevent civil war – Edward I of England.

When Edward was young his father had given him

Gascony in France, Chester in England and as much of Wales as he could conquer. He had conquered a lot of it, and helped his dad defeat rebellious barons, and fought in the Holy Land on a crusade of his own. As England's king he had curtailed Church property (he thought it owned too much) and deported all England's Jews in ships that landed them on Dogger Bank to be drowned by the rising tide. (He thought they owned too much.) In 1295 he established Britain's first modern government, convening at Westminster a parliament of lords, clergy, and representatives of shire and town to raise money for his wars. His legal and fiscal civil service was there to help them. This left Edward free to handle military business – he held Gascony as vassal of French King Philip and meant to break that vassalage, but first he accepted the Scottish invitation to choose a new king, and met their nobles at the frontier.

Before choosing he asked them all to swear allegiance to him. This would make the next Scottish king his vassal, but all the most powerful claimants swore at once because (1) they would lose their chance to be king if they did not; (2) because he would support the winner if the others ganged against him; (3) because they were used to swearing allegiance to him in England where he could deprive them of their English estates. The other nobles followed their example because (1) some of them had English estates too; (2) because earlier Scots kings had sworn allegiance to English ones for the sake of peace without making a difference to how Scotland was ruled; (3) because Edward had arrived with a large, well-equipped thoroughly disciplined army, which Scotland lacked.

The king Edward chose was John Baliol, later nicknamed *Toom Tabard*, Scottish for *Empty Coat*. In the records of his first parliament he appears to be an effective king, but the English legal system soon scooped him hollow.

After Baliol's coronation Edward announced that, to ensure justice in Scotland, from now on Westminster was the supreme court of appeal. In 1293 Macduff (descended from the thane who defeated Macbeth) lost a case in Scotland so took it to Westminster where lawyers and judges were glad to see him – rich clients pay big fees. The Westminster court summoned John Baliol before it to defend the Scottish court's decision, treating him like the sheriff of an English county. Baliol came to Westminster and said English judges had no legal authority over Scotland's king. The judges offered to adjourn the case. Baliol refused the offer because accepting it meant accepting the authority of the court. The judges said refusal showed contempt of court and sentenced Baliol to a fine of his three chief castles and towns. He changed his mind, accepted the adjournment, returned to Scotland.

Which proves you can't resist London inside London.

I will not give the dreary details of how Baliol signed a defensive alliance with Philip of France – how Edward attacked and butchered the people of Berwick and the Scots earls ravaged Tyneside – how the small Scottish army was smashed – how Baliol retreated as all his castles and towns were taken – how he surrendered, apologized, was publicly *uncrowned* and sent south with the official Scottish king-making apparatus: sandstone block to sit on, crown for head et cetera. Under feudal law Edward was now the only legal king of Scotland and therefore king of all Britain. But the Scots had only been lightly feudalized.

Edward put English regiments in the main Scottish

castles, put governors he could trust in the main towns, provided English garrisons to defend them supported out of local taxation. He ordered all Scotland's nobility to not just swear but *sign* a huge oath of allegiance to him which acknowledged they would be wicked traitors if they broke it. They signed. So did the chief citizens of the towns. Only three bishops signed and as Scotland had eight bishops this showed the Church could not be trusted. In Westminster Edward made a law that all vacancies in the Scottish church should henceforth be filled by Englishmen, then he felt free to tackle France.

Robert Wishart, bishop of Glasgow, was a churchman who had signed the grand declaration of loyalty. According to a contemporary reporter a year later he and other signers "caused a certain bloody man, William Wallace, who had formerly been chief of brigands in Scotland, to revolt against the king, and assemble the people in his support". Wallace was a small landowner driven to revolt by one of the injustices which are bound to happen under military occupations. Taking advantage of the geography that made Scotland poor – the wilderness between fertile districts – he attacked English garrisons one at a time, helped by the common people . . .

PUBLISHER: Please stop, I've seen the film –

AUTHOR: . . . and helped by the churchmen, spiritually and materially. Before Wishart emerged as a supporter of independence Edward gave him timbers to build a steeple for Glasgow Cathedral. Wishart gave them to Wallace for use as battering rams. Wallace cleared English garrisons from the lowlands while Moray, another young guerilla fighter, did so in the north. When nearly all the English soldiers had retreated into the big royal castles Wishart got Wallace knighted and proclaimed Guardian of the Scottish Commons. Had Scotland's nobility now joined Wallace wholeheartedly the fight for independence would have been won in two or three years. Snobbery, ambition and greed made it last sixteen.

Bruce and Comyn supported Wallace half-heartedly because he was a commoner leading an army of commoners. Wallace was fighting to restore John Baliol to the throne, and Comyn and Bruce wanted to be king. And of course they were likely to lose their English estates! Edward arrived with his usual professional army which soon smashed the front lines of Wallace's commoners. The noble cavalry officers behind them retreated, sent their apologies to Edward, were forgiven and swore allegiance to him a third time – English rulers often forgave treason when committed by one of their own class, a charming trait that persists to this day. Wallace was captured, tried for treason at Westminster, found guilty (though he had never sworn allegiance to Edward) and slowly tortured to death in accordance with an Anglo-Norman legal recipe. For a third time Edward went off to France thinking Scotland was finally his.

Scotland made it impossible for Edward to concentrate on his French business. The pope declared Scotland was a separate nation which Edward should leave alone. Bruce and Comyn now knew that if one stood aside the other could gain the whole kingdom in place of his English estates. They met to discuss the matter in Dumfries High Kirk. Bruce settled the argument by stabbing Comyn to death and six weeks later had himself crowned king of Scotland at Scone. Edward could never forgive him now! Bruce lost his English estates for ever, had to abandon his Scottish ones, for years had no chance of fighting on horseback like an Anglo-Norman nobleman. But he was Scottish born and his mother had been a Gael. He knew the language and went native, fighting a guerrilla war like Wallace and Guevara, avoiding pitched battles but steadily recapturing English garrisons with local support. He had an advantage over Wallace: noblemen could serve him without shame. Edward was told that, despite vengeance taken on Bruce's followers "the multitude wishing to confirm him in his kingship was increasing day by day". The clergy were supporting Bruce all over the north. The bishop of Moray said it was as virtuous to fight the English for Bruce as to fight the Saracens in the Holy Land.

No wonder Edward lost his temper and burned Scottish abbeys, unusual conduct then for a Christian king. He died leading another invasion force into the north. Extorting promises to the bitter end he made his son swear to carry his bones with the army until Scotland was finally conquered. Instead Edward II had his father suitably buried in Westminster Abbey under a monument with MALLEUS SCOTORUM carved on it, meaning Hammerer of Scots.

PUBLISHER: Why should such mediaeval politics matter today?

AUTHOR: Because our Scottish MPs are in the same state as the Scottish barons who swore allegiance to King Edward.

PUBLISHER: Explain that!

AUTHOR: For years Bruce, Comyn, Baliol and the others co-operated with Edward, Hammerer of Scots, because it gave them secure places and incomes in England. They also trusted him to keep Scotland for them. He commanded England, Ireland, Wales and much of France – surely he could keep Scotland for them? He could not. As the Scots commoners broke away it gradually became clear that the Scots barons would lose their Scottish property unless they joined them.

Today many Scots MPs (chiefly Labour ones) have enjoyed good salaries for years by their attachment to Westminster Palace (sometimes called "the best club in Europe") in jobs which allow them cosy adjacent apartments. By supporting a Great British Political System they have had to exercise their brains less than English MPs who are pestered, bullied and bribed to work for English constituents, deputations and the City of London. Scots MPs now know most of their electorate want home rule – they can no longer ignore it. Their problem is now to keep their seats in the best club in Europe without losing ground in Scotland. For nearly twenty years Scottish barons hung around Edward's court at Westminster with a similar problem, and Bruce was one of these hangers-on.

4
A KIND OF FREEDOM

THE KINGDOMS OF EUROPE belonged to a few great families who gained territory through marriage, inheritance and warfare, making the continent a political patchwork whose joins ignored the common sense of geological, linguistic and cultural frontiers. Owners of this patchwork stopped Germany and Italy getting territorial unity until well into the nineteenth century. The Bannockburn victory of 1314 made Scotland the first European state to have territorial unity under one ruler chosen by his subjects.

The novelty of this is shown in the Declaration of Arbroath, a letter to the pope. In 1320 he was a Frenchman from Guyenne, then an English territory, and excommunicated everyone in Scotland who would not take Edward II as their overlord. The Abbot of Arbroath wrote a reply on behalf of the "barons and freeholders and the whole community of the realm of Scotland". It was signed on behalf of the community by the noble families who had signed oaths of allegiance to Edward I, and by highland chiefs and Scandinavian Earls of Orkney and Caithness who had never signed.

The Declaration said that since ancient times the Scots had been free to choose their own kings; that this freedom, like all freedoms, was a gift of God; that if Robert Bruce were ever weak enough to swear allegiance to the English king they would dismiss him and choose someone else. It also said the pope would weaken his authority if he disagreed – "which God forbid".

It is easy to sentimentalize over the Declaration of Arbroath, but as a legal document signed by representatives of the Scottish community it is as revolutionary as the American Declaration of Independence. Note that King Robert the Bruce did not sign it. Those who did declared that he, the feudal owner of all Scotland, was a replaceable magistrate chosen by *all* Scots to protect their freedom. This meant that the ultimate owners of the Scottish *land* were the people living there.

PUBLISHER: Are you suggesting the Declaration legalizes land nationalization?

AUTHOR: The Scottish commoners had nationalized their landowners by making them abandon property in England and France. This was as far as nationalization could go in those days. It is not nationalization as the British government practises it when it compulsorily purchases Scottish land for use as nuclear weapons bases; but if the Declaration of Arbroath was retained as the founding charter of a restored Scottish nation then a democratically elected parliament could surely use it to give crofters and tenants more rights to the land and property they use.

PUBLISHER: Keep to the fourteenth century! Did the new, free Scotland become peaceful and prosperous again?

AUTHOR: No. England still claimed to rule it so raids and counter-raids continued between the two lands for many generations and most hurt the economy of the smaller nation. Scottish raids never touched the fertile plains around London but Scotland's most fertile ground was just south of Edinburgh where English raids kept wasting it again and again. The Scots often destroyed their own crops to stop them feeding invaders.

PUBLISHER: Very noble! The ravaging of the people, by the people, for the people.

AUTHOR: What else could they do?

PUBLISHER: If they had submitted to living in Scotlandshire ruled from London their lives would certainly have been more peaceful and probably better-off. You've admitted their kings were as selfish as England's. What good did the Scottish commoners get out of their nation's independence? Did it make *them* more independent?

AUTHOR: Yes. They had the right to openly scratch where they itched. Froissart, French chronicler of European chivalry, came to Scotland in the fourteenth century and was struck by the bad manners of the peasants. If a nobleman rode over a field the men who worked it screamed and yelled at him to get off, unlike the peasants of England and France whose lords had every right, in custom and law, to ride rough-shod and hawk and hunt over peasants' land without let or hindrance. This does not prove Scotland was democratic: it shows the Scots lairds and nobility respected the fact that commoners supported them out of crops which barely kept the commoners alive.

English imperialism forced Scotland and France into frequent alliances so French troops sometimes visited Scotland to attack England from the north. Few of them liked their uncouth allies. In the statutes of the French nobility there was a "Right of Plunder" allowing the military class, when short of money, to grab poultry, pigs, grain et cetera from peasants without paying for it. Two hundred hungry French soldiers from one such expedition tried to plunder a district of Scottish farmers who counter-attacked and killed some of them. In other lands this would have been treated as a peasants' revolt. The Scottish government ignored the complaints of their French allies who were given food and lodging in Edinburgh, but not allowed back to France before paying heavily for them. This persuades me that the common people also enjoyed some of the freedom asserted in the Declaration of Arbroath. There is another reason.

Good writing withers under tyrannies, as Russia under Stalin and Germany under Hitler proved. A comparison of English and Scottish literature shows the same thing.

The Norman conquest destroyed early English literature and a new one was impossible before rulers and ruled started talking the same language. This happened between 1330 and 1370 when the Black Death killed between a third and a half of the population. People of every rank died but in England the deaths of the poorer sort caused the biggest upheaval. Workers struck for higher wages and got them. Warfare and the building of cathedrals and palaces halted. Widespread debates began as labourers, gentry, clergy and traders jockeyed for power from positions of something like equality, and English literature was reborn. The great works of the English middle period were written between 1360 and 1400: *The Cloud of Unknowing*, *Sir Gawain and the Green Knight*, Langland's *Piers Plowman*, the poems and tales of Chaucer, Wyclif's English translation of the Bible, were written within forty years. So was *The Bruce*, the first epic poem in Scottish vernacular. This great period of writing was ended in England by censorship following the peasants' revolt, a rising of commoners against a poll tax created to finance warfare with France. It was partly led by worker priests and students from Oxford. After being bloodily suppressed a law was passed forbidding the teaching of reading and writing to children of labourers. All who preached in public had to be licensed by bishops. Owning Wyclif's English Bible became a crime for anyone not a bishop or nobleman and *Piers Plowman*, a poem describing corruption in Church and state while lamenting the plight of the poor, was banned by act of parliament.

There was no poll tax in Scotland, no peasants' revolt, a ban on Wyclif's Bible was the only censorship, so the period of fine writing that began with the epic of Barbour's *Bruce* lasted till the tumults of the Reformation a century and a half later. In this period was written *The Kingis Quair* by James I, the poems of Dunbar, Henryson's *Testament of Cresseid*, Gavin Douglas's translation of the *Aeneid*, Blind Hary's *Wallace*. It culminates in Sir David Lindsay's *Ane Pleasant Satyre of the Thrie Estaitis* publicly performed before the Scottish king, lords and commons. This verse play makes brilliant comedy of how a corrupt king, clergy and burgher class exploit John the Common Weal – the peasant farmer whose work supports them all, and has nobody to support him but Divine Correction, an angel of God. Langland's *Piers Plowman* had said this in a longer and far more Christian poem, yet his book was banned. A thing about this play is that the hero, King Humanity, is not just the supreme power in the state, he is also the character called Everyman in English miracle plays. This surely supports my reading of the Arbroath Declaration. Divine Correction teaches King Humanity to know John the Common Weal is his most important subject.

If we remember that the Scottish population in this period hardly exceeded half a million, and half of those used Gaelic as a first language, it is clear that many things must have combined to let this turbulent little nation add a wealth of imaginative poetry to European literature:

but nobody who has read some of that literature can doubt that a freedom of thought and speech linking every social rank was the most important.

PUBLISHER: Nobody prevents freedom of thought and speech in Britain today. Why should an old literature which hardly anyone can read nowadays matter to your argument?

AUTHOR: It shows that a small independent nation is capable of a rich culture.

5
REFORMATIONS

SCOTLAND'S THIN SOIL MEANT that most Scots lived close to famine so third sons – sometimes even second sons – often had to leave. Poverty had trained them to live upon little, grab the leavings of others and be alert for any opening, hence a French saying that rats, mice and Scots existed everywhere. Like the Swiss who were also bred on thin-soiled land many became mercenary soldiers. The Scots scholars found places abroad in the universities and bureaucracies of that grand multinational corporation and welfare state, the Catholic Church.

Like all secure old wealthy organizations the Church acquired many parasites and corrupt practices, so age after age reformers kept recalling it to the original idea of the Jewish founder: God is love. The partial successes of these reformers often got them sainted, made the Church wealthier than ever and made more and more statesmen envious of it. Edward the Hammerer tried taxing it by asking bishops and abbots to sit in parliament with the representatives of town and country. They dodged taxation by staying away. In Chaucer's day English statesmen had thought of privatizing that wealth but the peasants' revolt made them think again – arguments against the Church's worldly wealth had equal force against the private wealth of statesmen, so Church and state had united to hold down the masses.

Scottish nobles did not want it because the Scottish Church was in their power. Though it now owned half Scotland's wealth the king taxed it and filled its highest offices as he pleased, buying the support of strong families by granting them bishoprics, making his illegitimate sons abbots of great monasteries if they were old enough, financial managers of them (with the help of smart accountants) if they were not. The only folk who suffered under this system were badly paid local priests and their parishioners. In burghs enriched by trade a new middle class had begun making schools and hospitals for themselves without Church aid. It was in this class of people and their parish priests that reforming ideas eventually took hold, but Martin Luther's new Church appealed to nobody in Scotland.

In 1517 a Florentine pope rebuilding Rome's grandest cathedral raised funds by getting ecclesiastical brokers to sell cheap passports out of purgatory. Martin Luther, Augustine monk, publicly protested, then went on to denounce everything he found no sanctions for in the Bible – transubstantiation, clerical celibacy, papal authority and monastic estates. Many honest folk adopted his faith and many local magnates used it as a reason to seize Church property. But as before in England, the call to resist an oppressive Church caused a peasants' revolt against oppressive lords: whereupon Luther sprang to their defence saying, "The princes of this world are God's, the common people are Satan's . . . I would rather suffer a prince doing wrong than a people doing right." Yet many Christian princes still thought Luther was a low-class troublemaker, and Henry VIII of England being one of these.

Henry's father enriched the English Crown by raising money for wars he avoided fighting, so the young prince started life with great advantages. He married a Spanish princess when Spain had the world's biggest empire. His Church and state were managed by Cardinal Wolsey, an international negotiator who persuaded Spain, France, Germany and the papacy to sign a treaty with England against the Turks. It seemed possible that Wolsey might become the next pope and crown Henry the Holy Roman Emperor of all Christendom – an intoxicating dream. For a while the only disturbance of peaceful Europe seemed to be Martin Luther so Henry wrote a stern pamphlet against him and was rewarded with the papal title of Faith's Defender. That is why the initials FD still appear on British coins after the monarch's name.

Then England and France went to war again, and Henry wanted to divorce his Spanish wife because she could not give him a male heir, and the pope would not grant a divorce because Spain was his greatest ally. So the Faith's Defender declared himself pope of the Catholic Church in England, got divorced from wife 1 by the Archbishop of Canterbury and married wife 2 almost at once.

As a Catholic but non-Roman king Henry showed hatred of all extremists by burning in the same fire Catholics who preferred the pope in Rome and Protestants who denied transubstantiation. He also got middle-class support by first nationalizing monastic property (that is, seizing the revenues for the Crown) then privatizing it – selling that land cheap to professional people. This practically abolished the Catholic welfare state in England. A huge increase of homeless beggars followed, so tough laws were passed to make life hard for them.

PUBLISHER: Are you deliberately drawing a parallel between England then and Britain now?

AUTHOR: There are similarities, but Henry's efforts to take over Scotland are not among them, unless you count his success in depriving that nation of dependable government. Scotland being kingless, Henry proposed that his young son Edward marry the infant Mary, Queen of Scots. This would have made Henry the legal ruler of all Britain. The Scots evaded that proposal. Mary's French mother had no intention of having her daughter marry a heretic, and sent her to Paris where at the age of four she married the Crown Prince of France. Scotland's government was now in the hands of the French Queen Mother and Cardinal Beaton, head of the Scottish Church. Henry VIII and his successors *destabilized* that government – the modern word is appropriate.

English invasions looted and burned monasteries and churches to an extent which made the raids of Edward I look like pious restraint. Unable to garrison the whole country the English occupied three coastal forts which could be provisioned from England – Scotland had no navy. The Queen Mother counterbalanced these troops with French soldiers who occupied the port of Leith. For years Scottish politics were ruled by the jockeying of semi-Protestant nobles in the pay of England and semi-Catholic nobles in the pay of France. The word *semi* cannot be avoided because they kept changing sides when it gave them an advantage. But both sides tightened their grip on what had been Church lands because the dependence of the higher clergy on the nobility had left them too feeble to keep hold of it. Cardinal Beaton was the only patriotic churchman with strength to negotiate a path between England and France. Alas, he burned a Protestant preacher for heresy, one of those sent into Scotland with English aid. Some Protestant lairds for Fife broke into Beaton's castle and murdered him.

PUBLISHER: I'm sorry, but I must interfere again on the reader's behalf. What is the point of all this information?

AUTHOR: It explains how the ancient Catholic welfare state got dismantled by noble privatizers who left nothing for the "community of the realm" (as the Arbroath Declaration called it) but the necessity of organizing their own social services. The simplest way to do this was through Calvinism, which suited independent folk who expected little or nothing from nobility and could afford to spend little or nothing on hierarchies. John Knox was Scotland's leading Calvinist. England was now ruled by Queen Elizabeth. She ruled the English Church through Anglican bishops and detested Calvinism as DEMOCRATICAL and therefor detested John Knox. But she let her prime minister, Lord Cecil, correspond with him because Knox opposed the Scottish Catholic party.

Knox was wholly lacking in spiritual generosity. Like Luther, Torquemada, Lenin and Hitler he knew that all who disagreed with him were stupidly or deliberately evil. This certainty, along with courage, cunning, strong language and the will to utter it made him a political force. "Burn the trees and the crows will fly!" he said, exciting crowds to loot and destroy the houses of preaching friars who were his main competitors, so these houses were destroyed. In his *History of the Reformation in Scotland* he describes the murder of Cardinal Beaton as "merry work" thinking it a splendid stroke of satire that afterwards a Protestant pissed in the corpse's mouth. Such Calvinist rhetoric led to the destruction of church organs, stained-glass windows and beautiful carving – maybe as much as the armies of Henry VIII destroyed. The great achievement of reformers who made Knox their chief spokesman was *The Book of Discipline* issued by the first General Assembly of the reformed Kirk in 1560. It proposed a welfare state for the entire Scottish nation. There was nothing like it in British politics before the Beveridge Report of 1942.

It proposed that ministers of religion be elected by their congregations from trained clergymen, with elected elders to assist them. Clergy and elders would care for the poor and provide schooling for the entire parish – boys and girls, children of lairds and labourers. No child would be deprived of schooling because a parent wanted the work of their hands. From parish schools the best scholars would go to burgh schools where they would learn Latin, and thence to universities where they would train for law, arts or medicine, or for the Kirk of Scotland ministry – so the educational cycle would perpetuate itself. This faith in mass education came from believing nobody could be an intelligent Christian or citizen if they could not read and discuss the Bible – the Word of God. This teaching was planned in opposition to that of England where Oxford and Cambridge trained sons of nobility for places in the Anglican hierarchy. The Scots system was deliberately anti-hierarchic. Bursaries for poor scholars and teachers' wages were to be paid from the former revenues of the Catholic Church.

But Scots nobles who had confiscated the monastic estates wanted all the revenues for themselves – many of their descendants hold these lands to the present day. In his old age John Knox denounced the new landowners as worse than abbots and monks – the latter knew they should be helping the commoners and sometimes did. The new men lived shamelessly for themselves.

PUBLISHER: So the Scottish Reformation – like the English one – did the poorer people no good?

AUTHOR: It did some good. The idea that schooling should be free for ALL classes of children was widely accepted and partly acted upon. Many parishes created the primary schools John Knox wanted and several burghs did maintain secondary schools. Money from the Crown and acts of parliament strengthened these, so Scottish universities were never as inaccessible to the working class as Oxford and Cambridge. The Calvinist Netherlands, Switzerland and Scandinavia achieved similar schooling, but England's Church and state opposed education of children of labourers for centuries. When Henry VIII legalized the printing of English Bibles he forbade it to women and tradesmen. Even in the late nineteenth century English cabinet ministers were arguing against state-funded schooling for working-class children – it would make them unmanageable! And for a century and a half the children of Scottish weavers, shepherds and tradesmen had been enlarging the British empire by their achievements as linguists, inventors, doctors, explorers . . .

PUBLISHER: You're starting to rave. Have a cup of tea and cool down.

AUTHOR: A good idea.

6
UNITING BRITISH CROWNS

SCOTTISH EMIGRANTS WITH MARTIAL SKILL were employed by every nation in the European wars of religion, but during the reigns of Elizabeth I and James VI no battles were fought on the English mainland. For forty-five years Elizabeth kept herself and her country free of European politics by not marrying – she enjoyed flirting with foreign powers but was a resolute virgin. On her death the English Church and state wanted a king who would not disturb their property, a Protestant with no commitments outside Britain, so they gave the job to Jamie VI of Scotland. It is a pity he took it.

It is a great pity he took it. A king who dreaded warfare yet loved hunting, a pedantic scholar who doted on handsome young men but hated washing his hands, he had controlled a headstrong Scots nobility and Kirk with nothing but his wits, patience and help from people sick of political tumult. He had given them twenty years of central government but it had been a struggle and had not made him rich. When giving banquets to foreign ambassadors he had to borrow gold plate from neighbours and sometimes ask guests to supply their own food. Scottish trade had begun to prosper, his people had come to like him but he was glad to get away. Ruling Scotland from London was more comfortable.

PUBLISHER: As with the modern Scottish MP?

AUTHOR: Yes. In London he ruled England, Wales and Ireland too, so felt much more important.

He now had a good civil service under him, a rich treasury, a House of Lords and bishops who let him spend as he pleased as long as he protected their estates. The only danger to these came from Ireland. England had been conquering that land for centuries and none of the traditional methods listed by Niccolo Machiavelli had worked.

The best way to exploit a land without living there is through tax farming. You make native rulers richer by giving them power to tax their subjects more heavily than they could without you, as long as they pay you most of the takings. This only works in a land with a monetary system, and Ireland had practically none. Its trade was mostly barter, its taxes paid in produce England did not want. Another tactic is to find a strong native clan and isolate it from the rest by paying it to work as your police force. Jamie and later British kings did that in the Scottish highlands with the Campbells of Argyll, but it did not work as well in Ireland. The Irish persisted in hating the English more than each other, so Norman, Plantagenet, Tudor overlords before Jamie's reign, Cromwellian and Hanoverian rulers after it, kept resorting to general massacres which left the winners sickened and exhausted, the Irish as Irish as ever. And most Irish were still Catholic! If a Catholic counter-revolution came to the British mainland the Irish might send in an army across the narrow channel dividing Ulster from Kintyre and Galloway. A large body of English settlers might have held Ulster down, but very few English wanted to settle in a hostile and much poorer land. Bearing all this in mind Jamie did what could only be done by a Scottish king ruling Ireland with an English army: he colonized Ulster.

This was the first and largest of all state-assisted

Scottish emigration. Two thirds of northern Ireland were confiscated by the British crown. The natives were ordered to leave or remain in the condition of servants, and their land was given to Protestant settlers from Britain, the great mass of these being Scots Calvinists. According to the English historian John Richard Green:

> *In its material results the plantation of Ulster was undoubtedly a brilliant success . . . the foundations of the economic prosperity which has raised Ulster high above the rest of Ireland in wealth and intelligence were undoubtedly laid in the confiscation of 1610. . . . The evicted natives withdrew sullenly to the lands which had been left them by the spoiler; but all faith in English justice had been torn from the minds of the Irishry, and the seed had been sown of that fatal harvest of distrust and disaffection, which was to be reaped through tyranny and massacre in the age to come.*

Green wrote that in 1874. He was referring to tyrannies and massacres in the seventeenth and eighteenth centuries, not the twentieth. But with the backing of the Ulster Protestants the big Anglo-Irish landowners broke the power of ancient clan chieftains and brought their land into the English mercantile system.

When King James (that royalest of emigrants) signed the act of confiscation he believed he was welding three nations into one, not splitting them into four. He died in 1625 believing he had succeeded. The civil wars which followed proved him wrong.

They began with a Scottish Covenant against Charles I's attempt to impose the English episcopal system here. Scottish mercenaries hurried home from the continent to join the Covenanters' army of resistance. The king was defeated in the north, and soon after went to war with his parliament in England. The English parliament asked the Scots for aid and received it on condition that England adopt the Scottish Calvinist system. Aid was accepted, the king defeated, but Cromwell soon dispensed with a parliament which had made promises it could not keep. The Scots delusion that they could change England's religion was stupider than Charles's episcopal plans for Scotland. These stupidities happened because the executive head of both nations lived inside the southern one: a bad set-up from which Scotland suffered most. Without an internal authority holding her together she fell or tore herself apart. At one time she contained four armies: a Scottish army from the Lothians and Fife fighting for king and Covenant, a partly Irish and partly highland army fighting for king against Covenant, a small army of south-west Covenanters fighting everybody to make Britain a Calvinist republic, and a mainly English army fighting for Cromwell's commonwealth. Cromwell won.

The restoration of the Stuart monarchy after the Commonwealth did Scotland no good. Charles II ruled his northern kingdom through a small clique of Scottish sycophants who plundered it for their own financial advantage. At one time they tried one of their enemies for treason, punished him with a huge fine, and after he had paid it tried him for the same crime in a second trial which condemned him to death. This lawlessness masquerading as law-and-order became another attempt to force the English episcopal system upon all Scotland – Charles II eventually sent his brother James to Edinburgh to enforce it, which complicated matters. Though James tried to force an English Protestant liturgy on the Scots he was a Roman Catholic. Covenanting farmers and weavers in the south and west deserted the government-controlled kirks to hold services in the open air, so many were spied out and shot. It is natural to sympathize with these victims of intolerant government – they were poor, brave and victimized. But whenever their combinations got them a brief advantage they treated the women and children of their enemies with the same intolerant cruelty.

When Charles II died his brother James became king of Britain, and to make his own Catholicism legal for others proclaimed universal toleration of EVERY religion. Only the Catholics were pleased. Episcopalian English and Presbyterian Scots united to expel James and make King Billy, a Dutch Calvinist, the chief executive of Britain and the British Faith's Defender. In these circumstances King Billy agreed to defend the Protestant Episcopal Church in England and Ireland but the Protestant Presbyterian Church in Scotland.

Yet by 1695 it was obvious to most Scots that having a king in London did not benefit them. The lords and gentry in Scotland's parliament could only deal with their ruler through a small number in the monarch's pay. Meanwhile King Billy, and after him Queen Anne, signed English acts of parliament which strengthened English colonies, English trade and the English stock exchange in ways which excluded Scotland. English fleets traded with colonies and plantations containing Scottish overseers and settlers, but which excluded Scottish ships; nor could the Scots trade freely with Europe because England was usually at war with either Holland or France, her chief mercantile competitors. When James VI had gone south over ninety years before he had told the Scots he was going from one part of an island to another to secure their greater comfort. The only folk made more comfortable had been some other clever émigrés who went south too. William Paterson was the most successful. Here is the entry on him in *Chambers Biographical Dictionary*:

> PATERSON, *William (1658–1719)*
> *Scottish financier, founder of the Bank of England, born at Skipmyre farm, Tinwald, Dumfriesshire, and spent some years in the West Indies. Returning to Europe, he promoted his Darien Scheme in London, Hamburg, Amsterdam (where he worked for the Revolution of 1688) and Berlin, made a fortune by commerce in London, founded the Hampstead Water Company in 1690, projected the Bank of England, and was one of its first directors in 1694. At Edinburgh, as a strong advocate of free trade, he talked the whole nation into his Darien Scheme.*

7
UNITING BRITISH PARLIAMENTS

PATERSON STARTED A SCOTTISH Trading Company which (like the Bank of England and East India Trading Company in London) would be supported by a parliament, but by Scotland's parliament. On a globe of the world he proved that by planting a colony across the isthmus of Panama Scotland could dominate the most profitable trade route in the world. With ports on the Atlantic and Pacific shores Scots merchants could reach every coast of north and south America, while opening routes across the Pacific to Asia. This would destroy the monopoly of the East India Company without breaking a single English law. Moreover, Darien was uninhabited! And the chief executive, King Billy himself in London, had recently passed a law that the royal navy would protect all British colonies on uninhabited coasts.

This scheme sounded so convincing that even London merchants joined it until the East India Company threatened to impeach them in the English parliament. The Darien Venture became wholly Scots. Lords, lairds, merchants and professional men became so patriotically hopeful that they invested half Scotland's money in Paterson's company – about £400,000. It is impossible to calculate the value of this money in modern terms, but multiplying by a hundred would almost certainly produce too small an equivalent, and at that time Scotland's population was one and a half million – it is now about five and a half. Of the money invested they lost roughly

£200,000. They should first have discovered why that part of Panama was uninhabited.

The Scottish emigrants sailed there and began building New Edinburgh, a port which did not last long enough to get its name printed on a map. The dank air was full of malaria. The settlers soon grew feverish and had to fight off Spaniards who attacked them from healthier parts of the coast. They asked King Billy in London for protection but he said he could not give it without disturbing the peace of Christendom. The Darien colony beat off the Spaniards once, begged help from nearby English colonies who refused it, eventually had to surrender. Paterson was one of the few hundred who got home, leaving about two thousand dead behind him and having lost a quarter of Scotland's capital.

But he had done his best, so the Scots blamed the English. This was illogical. Mosquitoes had been the main enemy. On the other hand, if the colony had been English the government in London would have forgotten that Spaniards were fellow Christians and driven them away. The magnates who ruled England had invited the Stuarts south because they thought them more manageable than other royal families. They had been mistaken. Taming the Stuarts had been a long, expensive struggle and having got a more amenable king they meant to use him. As Alexander Pope said, "A king may be a tool, a thing of straw; but if he serves to frighten our enemies it is well enough; a scarecrow is a thing of straw, but it protects the corn." And the English grandees were not anti-Scottish racists. When Paterson founded the Bank of England with the help of the London parliament he was their partner. When he founded the Scottish Company with the help of the Edinburgh parliament he was their competitor. He had been foolish to think a British king would help the City of London's competitors. Then the City of London suddenly gave Scottish pride another hard knock.

King Billy died. Queen Anne came to the throne and would certainly be the last Stuart monarch because she was middle-aged, childless, and other surviving Stuarts were all Catholics. Without consulting Scotland England's parliament decreed that the German Prince of Hanover would be king of Britain after her – he had promised to join the Church of England. London had asked them to accept King Billy – they had agreed because he was a Calvinist. They had gladly welcomed Queen Anne because she was a Stuart. By trying to impose George Hanover on them without consultation England's parliament was treating them as a province. So the Scottish parliament refused to recognize George Hanover as the king of Scotland, and for a while it seemed Scotland would be independent again. The mass of the Scottish people wanted that but democracy was centuries away. . . . Are you listening to me, Stephanie?

PUBLISHER: Yes. Why do you ask?

AUTHOR: Because I repeat, with emphasis, that *the Scottish people did not get the independence they wanted because democracy was centuries away.* Scotland's parliament represented and consisted of folk who had lost a quarter of Scotland's money through mismanaged speculation and hoped to get some back by trade with England – the threat to break with her was a bargaining ploy to make England drop her anti-Scottish customs barriers. Only one Scots parliamentarian, Fletcher of Saltoun, wanted true independence. He said Scotland should make herself a self-supporting republic like the Netherlands, with Scots emigration abolished by binding Scottish peasants to the estates where they were born, and every landlord fully employing his workers in agriculture, mining and manufacture by the newest methods. This suggestion was ignored. Commissioners went to London with Scottish terms for a new treaty of union. The Anglo-German king would be accepted in return for free trade with England and permission to keep the Presbyterian religion. In 1707 the commissioners came back with English terms for a very different treaty.

It proposed that the Scots parliament should swear allegiance to the king chosen by England, and make Scottish revenue officers pay Scots taxes into the English treasury, and abolish the Scottish Trading Company, and abolish itself, in return for which England would:

LET 45 SCOTTISH MPs JOIN 513 ENGLISH AND WELSH MPs IN WESTMINSTER.

LET 16 SCOTTISH LORDS JOIN 190 ENGLISH ONES IN WESTMINSTER.

LET SCOTLAND KEEP ITS ANCIENT LAWS AND LEGAL SYSTEM.

LET THE PRESBYTERIAN CHURCH REMAIN THE OFFICIAL CHURCH OF SCOTLAND.

GIVE AN IMMEDIATE CASH PAYMENT OF £398,085 AND 10 SHILLINGS.

This eccentric sum of money equalled the Scots investment in the Scottish Trading Company which was to be abolished. It was also the exact sum Scottish shareholders had lost on their Darien gamble. This was not exactly generous of England, since the English treasury would recover the cash by taxing Scotland after its parliament dissolved; nor did the Scots–English MP ratio of 45 to 513 fairly correspond to the number of Scots–English people – Cornwall had 43 MPs.

During the long debate on this Union treaty a spy of the English government judged that the Scottish people were fifty-to-one against. Churchmen denounced it; burghs petitioned against it; Glasgow, Dumfries and Edinburgh crowds rioted against it. Most of the Scottish parliament hated it too, but dreaded the alternative. The English had passed an Aliens Act to blockade all Scottish external trade if the Treaty was refused. There was also danger of warfare. England had plantations and factories in Ireland, America, Africa, India, and without straining its credit was fighting a successful war against France, now the richest power in Europe. When that war ended it would certainly have means to crush an independent Scotland. The union promised Scotland's rulers immediate peace and money in their pockets. So among the curses of the nation it should have defended Scotland's parliament voted itself out of existence by a large majority, with only a moment of hesitation caused by late delivery of promised cash. Here is the song Robert Burns wrote about the event nearly eighty years later:

Fareweel to a' our Scottish fame,
   Fareweel our ancient glory!
Fareweel even to the Scottish name,
   Sae fam'd in martial story!
Now Sark rins o'er the Solway sands,
   And Tweed rins to the ocean,
To mark where England's province stands;
   Such a parcel of rogues in a nation!

What guile or force could not subdue,
   Through many warlike ages,
Is wrought now by a coward few,

For hireling traitors' wages.
The English steel we could disdain,
Secure in valour's station,
But English gold has been our bane;
Such a parcel of rogues in a nation!

O would, ere I had seen the day
That treason thus could sell us,
My auld grey head had lien in clay,
Wi' Bruce and loyal Wallace!
But pith and power, till my last hour
I'll mak this declaration,
We're bought and sold for English gold;
Such a parcel of rogues in a nation!

The sixty-one lords and MPs who now represented their country migrated to London as a Scottish king had done a century earlier. The MP for the Dumfries Burghs, William Paterson, had worked to promote this Union after the failure of his Darien plan. The British parliament later awarded him £18,000. Though a bad colonizer he was still a financial genius.

Then the Independent Scottish Legal System discovered what poor Toom Tabard had discovered – in all important matters the Westminster lords over-rule it. This allowed the British parliament to give Scottish landlords the right to choose clergy for the Independent Presbyterian Scottish Kirk, thus starting a turmoil which eventually broke the Kirk in two. Meanwhile the British government spread taxation in a way which deliberately helped English trade and depressed Scotland's. English coal could enter Ireland duty-free, Scottish coal could not. England's main industry was wool so the government put a light export duty on it. Scotland's was linen so the government put a heavy duty on it. English brokers took shares in the Irish linen trade, got a government subsidy to expand it, and began buying Scottish flax for it. Scots MPs protested that ancient Scots law forbade the taking of flax from Scotland, since it would ruin the Scottish weavers. They pointed out that breaking that law broke the Treaty of Union. Here are replies they got from the Great British Government:

> *"Whatever are or may be the laws of Scotland, now she is subject to the sovereignty of England, she must be governed by English laws."*
>
> *"Have we not bought the Scots and the right to tax them?"*
>
> *"We have catcht Scotland and will keep her fast."*

In his book *The Lion in the North* John Prebble says,

> *"England's lack of sympathy for Scotland's particular needs seemed sometimes perverse and malicious, the triumphs of a small boy who is winning a game he has himself devised."*

He also says,

> *"For more than a quarter of a century it did seem as if Union were a greater disaster than the Darien Venture."*

Several English thought it had damaged their country too.

Since the sixty-one Scottish commoners and lords in Westminster were now unable to rule their own land they compensated themselves by getting all the money they could from bribery and jobbery. Like nowadays, private companies and pressure groups paid cash for votes, speeches and questions in the House. Most British

MPs were enriched that way but in the eighteenth century none so predictably as the Scots. That was, and is, bribery. Jobbery was getting salaried seats on the boards of English companies (still taken for granted nowadays) and putting relatives and supporters into the excise or post office, sometimes in return for cash. That kind of jobbery is nowadays replaced by posts in quangos – Quasi Autonomous Non-Governmental Organizations to promote equal opportunities for women, or privatize water, or do many other good, bad, but always lucrative things – and always outside electoral control. (In 1997 there are now more than 7500 such organizations dispersing more than £50 billion of public money.)

But to enjoy these perquisites the Westminster Scots needed strong Scottish managers at home to secure their parliamentary seats by bribing and jobbing the northern electors. The most efficient of these was Henry Dundas, nicknamed The Uncrowned King of Scotland. He ruled from 1775 to 1805 on the friendliest terms with every British prime minister in that period. He was only deposed when some of his fellow politicians felt that a little less corruption would not cause a revolution.

PUBLISHER: Who are the modern Henry Dundases?

AUTHOR: Heads of local Scottish Labour Parties who control our town councils. They defended the electoral base of Scottish Labour MPs by promoting the policies of Margaret Thatcher and John Major even more thoroughly than most local councils in England, Labour or Tory. None of these risked the fate of Ken Livingstone in the council of Greater London.

The English parliamentary system was based on competitive voting between electors and MPs mostly bribed by the court, the great landlords and the City of London.

There was enough open argument between these for European visitors to think England the most free nation in the world. Scots in the Houses of Lords and Commons found it most lucrative to vote for the King's party. Unlike his lazier father and grandfather George III wanted to rule Britain personally, and by sheer bribery and jobbery obtained a working majority in the Commons. That and the royal prerogative made his party stronger than any other for twelve years. He was a hard-working, obstinate, not personally vicious king but foolish and egoistic. He completely mishandled Britain's American colonies and bungled the subsequent war. When Whigs and Tories combined to defeat the King's Party the Scots sold their votes to Tories who offered most. This steady Scottish support for all that was most corrupt and entrenched in England drove John Wilkes, MP for Middlesex and Lord Mayor of London, to declare:

> *The River Tweed is the line of demarcation between all that is noble and all that is base – south of the river is all honour, virtue and patriotism – north of it is nothing but lying, malice, meanness and slavery. Scotland is a treeless, flowerless land, formed out of refuse of the universe, and inhabited by the very bastards of creation.*

He was venting his political frustration of course, but there was something mean in Scots parliamentarians who had sold the independence of their own people and now hired themselves out to those conspiring against the freedom of the English.

But throughout the eighteenth and nineteenth and twentieth centuries the British government encouraged one great Scottish industry: the export of people. An expanding and widespread financial empire needs soldiers. A working army uses up healthy men fast. Britain could never have defeated the French in France, Canada and India with recruits from the poor and unemployed of south Britain, a comparatively prosperous place. It employed German and Irish mercenaries of course, but these were not enough. From Scotland, especially the highland part, the British government soon recruited whole regiments with their commanding officers too.

8
DISASTER & RECOVERY

PUBLISHER: It's time you said something about Gaelic Scotland – the Scotland of the clans. So far you have said more about England and Ireland. Why?
AUTHOR: The differences between Scotland and other places seemed more important than an inner difference, one which the Reformation worsened.
PUBLISHER: But you've already stated that highland and lowland difference is geological, that the hunting, fishing, cattle-rearing highlanders were fiercer warriors than farmers and townsmen of the south.
AUTHOR: Yet the western Gaels had given Scotland its name and earliest kings and first Christian settlements, places where the Word of God was first written and sung. The early Church also wrote the vernacular poetry and chronicles of their own people – the earliest surviving literature of the Irish, Welsh and English. The wholesale destruction of monastic libraries in Scotland meant that hardly any ancient Gaelic vernacular literature survived before nineteenth-century scholars wrote it down from Gaels who had maintained the work of their poets by memory and word of mouth. Yet highlands and lowlands had something essential in common while both had a king and a parliament in Edinburgh. When first the king, then the parliament left for London the highland and lowland cultures became farther and farther apart, partly because the clans still had their own local governments, chiefs who mostly lived among them until 1745.

Once again France and England were at war. Once again the French government wanted Scotland to divert its continental opponents, so it landed Prince Charles Edward Stuart (a half-Polish young man) on a loyal part of the highlands. Less than half the clans rallied to him. He entered lowland Scotland, quickly defeated the small Hanoverian forces there and after enjoying some parties in Edinburgh marched into England. Few lowlanders joined his army. Why should they fight to put yet another Stuart on the London throne? With the possible exception of James VI they had done Scotland no good at all. When the highlanders found no English joined them either they sensibly went home. An English army followed and destroyed their army at Culloden, then butchered native civilians as a lesson to the rest and arrested all who remained of the beaten army along with possible sympathizers. Most of these prisoners were sold as slaves to America, but the main damage to Gaeldom was done through the clan chieftains who remained in alliance with the British government.

Under David I's feudal law the chiefs administered justice very much at their own discretion, but kinship had stopped them treating their people too savagely. Parliament now deprived the chiefs of their law-administering power, forcing them to work more closely with the government in London, but this gave them more, not less authority over their people. In the lowlands and England many commoners had firm rights to their homes and plots of land through purchase or rental. Clansmen had no such firm rights, so now the chiefs could make money out of their bit of Scotland in any way they pleased. In the nineteenth century this often meant forcing clansfolk out of their ancestral glens to places like Canada, because sheep were more profitable animals. When wool grew cheap because of imports from Australia it became more profitable to rent the land to foreigners on hunting holidays; but long before this happened the chiefs made full use of the loyalty their clansmen owed them as military leaders. They enlisted as colonels in the British army, formed regiments and fought for England (south Britons kept thinking of themselves as English) in France, Spain, America, Canada, India et cetera.

English generals found them excellent front-line troops. On commanding them against the Québecois General Wolfe wrote that it was a good idea to preserve English lives by expending those of former enemies. Slowly the highlanders began to see that their chiefs were no longer exactly their friends. After enlisting for a European war a regiment in Edinburgh Castle heard it would be posted to India. This meant an absence of many years, and deaths by disease on the voyage there and back were frequent. The regiment left the Castle for Arthur's Seat, camped there and threatened to disband unless given certain assurances. Their officers assured them they would not be sent to India. The regiment returned, was dispersed among other troops, had its ringleaders executed for mutiny. The rest were sent to India, most of them dying of disease on the way. I will quote John Prebble again:

> *The last tragedy of the clans may not be the slaughter of Culloden, but the purchase and wasteful expenditure of their courage by the southern peoples who had at last conquered them.*

But while the highlands were coming to these terms with the Great British government something more cheerful was happening in the lowlands. The disastrous thirty years following the Treaty of Union had taught lairds, craftsmen and tradesmen a lesson: they could only prosper by working together without the help of king and parliament. They started doing what Fletcher of Saltoun had advised. They made the Scottish lowlands a self-managing, middle-class republic. They formed local societies for the improvement of land, trade and science but especially land. Two thirds of land farmed nowadays in the Scottish lowlands has been reclaimed from moors by drainage, manuring and enclosures begun in the eighteenth century. In the south west some of these enclosures drove poor tenants off the soil, but less of this happened in Scotland than England because in Scotland more farms could be extended into wilderness. The great landlords, working mainly through Edinburgh lawyers, leased unproductive land at low rents to natives who worked to improve it. When they had done so the rents could be raised. If a tenant could not pay the higher rent he or his sons could be evicted to start work on poorer soil again. Robert Burns's father was a tenant farmer of this kind. He and his son struggled from one poor farm to another. The poet died young from the rheumatic illness got at the age of twelve while helping his dad bring in a difficult harvest. Thousands who were not great poets died early for similar reasons.

Despite the harshness of their lives the tenant farmers and tradesfolk of English-speaking Scotland bred a high proportion of scholars, discoverers and inventors between 1750 and the First World War because the Calvinist education had produced an unusually literate working class. It had also produced a fanatical, narrow-minded and superstitious clergy, but in 1720 these lost all credit by getting a student who doubted the divinity of Christ hanged for heresy, causing a nationwide reaction into sensible, secular tolerance. Education was no longer severely religious. Where there was no parish school a few tenant farmers might unite and hire a student to teach their children during university vacations. That is how knowledge of Shakespeare, Milton and the French language were added to Burns's acquaintance with Scottish ballads, the Bible and Blind Hary's *Wallace*. Similar contacts with a dominie or minister helped others of the Scottish working class into professions closed to all but the middle class in other nations.

But having gained professional skills only three ways forward existed for sons of the poor who did not themselves want to be ministers or dominies.

1 Employment by one of the prospering Glasgow trade companies. This often meant being posted as slave-driver to a sugar plantation in the West Indies, cotton or tobacco plantation in America. (Burns was leaving for Jamaica when news that his poems had made him famous turned him back.)
2 Employment through the patronage of the landlords and law lords who managed Scotland. (By such patronage Burns was made an exciseman when he could no longer support his family by poetry and farming.)
3 Employment by the English. (James Watt joined partnership with Matthew Bolton in Birmingham because only there could he get capital to make the steam engine he had conceived in Glasgow. William Murdoch, inventor of gas lighting, went to Manchester for the same reason. John Leyden, oriental philologist, served the British government as adviser to the governors of India and Java. Mungo Park explored the Niger for the African Association of London.)

Most of such men had studied under professors whose science and philosophy had put their universities far in advance of Oxford and Cambridge which chiefly existed to give sons of the wealthy a gloss of classical learning and train Anglican clergy. Since the death of Isaac Newton English science was mainly developed by the Royal Society in London and discussions between industrial experts in the midlands.

Though Scottish education was more modern than England's other social institutions were more primitive. Parliamentary elections had never changed the clique managing Scotland. Foreigners like Voltaire, Rousseau and Thomas Jefferson praised Edinburgh as an intellectual capital second to none, yet Scottish coalminers and salt-panners were hereditary serfs found nowhere else in Britain. Protestant landlords had acquired them when privatizing other properties of the Catholic Church, and a law of James VI had made it a crime to help a coalminer escape from his employment. Legal serfdom was abolished in 1799 but cannot have improved conditions at first. The miners knew no livelihood but hewing coal; their homes belonged to owners who could evict whole families if a breadwinner got other work; more than half a century passed before trade unions were legalized.

Toward the end of the eighteenth century, then, Scotland had three social classes detached from each other and without English equivalents. The worst off were highland military serfs and lowland industrial serfs. Almost disconnected from these was a middle class of highly literate tradesmen and tenant farmers whose professional superiors were the university lecturers and law lords in Edinburgh, the latter belonging to a European aristocracy of learning. But Scotland's landed aristocracy worked from town houses in London, regarded their homeland as English landowners regard their country estates, sent sons to Eton or Harrow, Oxford or Cambridge, where they learned to mingle with fashionable English society and strengthen their fortunes through marriage alliances with English fortunes. By such educations sons of the greatest highland chiefs learned to despise their own culture, making it easier for them later to apply Norman property laws against their people more sweepingly than had been seen in Britain since the days of William the Waster.

An uncomfortable separation will always exist between a hereditary class of wealthy owners and those who work on the land they own, or are their far less privileged neighbours. In Scotland this separation was once less embarrassing. In the first decades after parliamentary union many Scots lords, landed and legal, took pride in talking the speech of the commoners, which had also been the speech of the royal Stuarts before they travelled south. With every generation since then the speech difference increased until now the voices of the Scottish ruling class sound exactly like those of the English. The noise of such voices braying in parliament (for dominating accents are as liable to bray as lower-class voices to mumble) gives a majority of Scots the sensation of living under a foreign occupation; but I am sure many English feel that way too.

9
DEMOCRACY: AMERICAN DAWN

IN HIS *LIVES OF THE ENGLISH POETS* DR JOHNSON referred to Britain as one of those states "formed by accident and ruled by the passions of those who preside in them". It had no written constitution to inhibit those who presided there, but it had a hereditary king, a House of hereditary lords who presided over counties, a House of Commoners elected by smaller landowners.

Before 1832 about one in a hundred and twenty-five Scots householders could vote: their electoral districts had been established by James VI in 1587. English MPs were voted for by roughly one out of fifty householders: electoral districts had been established in 1395 by Edward, Hammerer of Scots. Some constituencies since then had been turned into pasture by the wool industry – the cathedral city of Sarum, for example, was now a great mound where sheep grazed. Those who owned the ground of an unpeopled constituency could choose MPs for it without troublesome elections. The rights to Sarum were bought by an ex-governor of Madras called Pitt and were inherited by his family, two of whom became prime ministers. Such constituencies strengthened the Tory or big landowners' party. Growing industries had also created new towns and cities without voices in the Commons, but men enriched through industry could become MPs by purchasing votes from a long-established town council or hereditary landlord. Such constituencies strengthened the Whig or big business party. In Scotland, however, all constituencies were in the pockets of Dundas and noble landlords. Newly rich Scots could only become MPs by purchasing boroughs in England.

Free elections could only happen where Whigs and Tories contested a seat with strong backing on each side. Since electors cast their votes in public such elections were riotous carnivals of open intimidation and bribery which proved the strength of English liberty. In Scotland candidates were selected by the national manager so hardly ever opposed. In Switzerland and the Netherlands elections were more sober affairs, and didn't happen elsewhere on the continent. Corruption in British politics was openly defended by corruptors and corrupted. They said, "It is as notorious as the sun at noonday!" – meaning, "This system keeps parliament in the power of the wealthy. It puts money in our pockets, has created the greatest trading empire on earth, and has driven our strongest competitors, the French, out of India and north America. Could a juster voting system have done so well?"

Old Corruption (as the British Constitution was nicknamed by its critics) took a hard knock in 1776. Our hereditary legislators would not let American colonists vote on how they were taxed, so thirteen colonies united to make a new nation without hereditary legislators. Their Declaration of Independence said:

We hold these truths to be self evident, that all men are created equal and endowed by their creator with certain unalienable rights; that among these are life, liberty and the pursuit of happiness. That to secure these rights, governments are instituted among men, deriving their just power from the consent of the

> *governed. That whenever any form of government is destructive of these ends, it is the right of the people to alter or abolish it.*

This changed the course of history.
PUBLISHER: No doubt. Why quote it?
AUTHOR: Because in it a prospective government offers terms of partnership to a prospective people. Like the Arbroath Declaration it announces the people's sovereignty in defence of freedom, but goes further in declaring each citizen should have equal rights. Earlier nations had been formed while repelling invasion, England under Alfred, Scotland under Bruce, but such rulers made no promises beforehand, except, perhaps, to their strongest supporters. Five years before the British army in north America surrendered Thomas Jefferson's words told supporters of the United States that they were fighting for a democracy where all would have equal voting rights.
PUBLISHER: All didn't get them! Women, Red Indians and slaves had no votes! The southern states kept slaves till the 1870s.
AUTHOR: True. And in the earliest elections the labouring classes were forbidden to vote by property qualifications. But Jefferson's prologue contradicted these limitations, urging voters with a sense of justice to abolish them. They eventually did.

The new federal republic stayed united because, black and red men apart, most Americans took male social equality for granted. In the first fifty years the earnings of industrious workmen, backwoods trappers, settled farmers, tradesmen and lawyers were not different enough to make class distinctions look like God's will or nature's decree. The USA had then no industrial cities, no slums or ghettos, no millionaires. Founders like Jefferson and Washington owned estates worked by slaves, yet with Mozart and Robert Burns they were Freemasons who subscribed to the brotherhood of man so felt guilty about slave-owning. Tom Paine, an English journalist fighting beside Washington, persuaded the Yankees that hereditary lordships and regalia were bad for democracy. Some citizens thought hereditary wealth might become as damaging as hereditary titles, and suggested a legal limit to the money an American could make out of his nation; but wealthy founders thought democracy required the pursuit of unlimited riches, so today social equality is mainly found in Scandinavian democracies.

The American Declaration also gave Ireland some political freedom. Since the early fourteenth century its parliament could pass no law that England's parliament did not authorize or dictate, and English troops were garrisoned close by to make sure of this. These troops were now needed to quell the Yanks. Ireland's parliament was allowed independence because, being a wholly Protestant body governing a mainly Catholic people, it was thought they would be too busy holding their country down to act independently. For exactly that reason several Irish parliamentarians wanted Catholic MPs beside them and formed a Society of United Irishmen in which Catholics, Anglicans and Calvinists worked for the common cause. Need of parliamentary change was also felt in England.

Whig and Tory MPs knew that the king's servants in the House of Lords and bribed sycophants in the Commons had lost Britain's colonies in America. They needed more middle-class support to defeat a government which seemed unable to learn from mistakes, so invited the middle class to form societies demanding electoral reform. Societies were formed but not all were confined to the gentry the parliamentarians wanted. The Society of the Friends of the People admitted craftsmen and tradesmen, and when its emissaries came to Scotland they were astonished by an influx of handloom weavers, then the largest, most prosperous and best educated part of the Scottish working class. Among their favourite reading was Tom Paine's book *Rights of Man.* This argued that people of every nation would benefit as much as the Yankees if they stopped paying taxes to support a parasitic king, lords and established Church which kept power by bribery, jobbery and military action against other nations. Paine said that the nation's revenues (which were then collected through a value-added tax on candles, shoe leather, soap, glass windows and other things the poorest part of the nation felt they needed) should be used to pay for old-age pensions, good schooling for everyone, and child benefits paid directly to the mother. These ideas made sense to artisans in south Britain too, but more to Scots who could take no pride in the proximity of the king and his lords, and had not been bribed by them.

So the northern class division widens. Parliamentary Scots are so completely in the pay of the dominant English that the English despise them, while the Scottish working class grows more radical and resentful of such government.

Scotland's Friends of the People had middle-class organizers. One of them, a Glasgow lawyer called Thomas Muir, corresponded with George Washington, with Wolfe Tone who led the United Irishmen, with members of the French parliament – because at last France was ruled by an assembly of commoners. The French nation was now so bankrupt that poor King

Louis could not pay his soldiers' wages. Not knowing what to do about this he had called together the first French parliament in 175 years to advise him.

PUBLISHER: Was this the start of the French revolution?

AUTHOR: Yes. Like the American Senates and United Irishmen its members were upper or middle class, but felt themselves elected to act for the whole nation.

PUBLISHER: Thomas Muir was in touch with its leaders?

AUTHOR: That revolution had thousands of leaders and yes, Muir was in touch with some.

PUBLISHER: So he was an international conspirator?

AUTHOR: The managers of Scotland thought so. They arrested him for sedition. He was tried in Edinburgh under a judge who told the jury Muir was guilty before the trial began. Muir was in one of the earliest batches of convicts sent to Botany Bay. An American naval vessel helped him escape from Australia. Despairing of English parliamentary reform he at last wanted Scotland to proclaim a democratic republic of its own. Maybe that is why the French National Assembly made him a member before he died.

PUBLISHER: Which *proves* he was an international conspirator!

AUTHOR: Or organizer. The difference between conspirator and organizer is one of viewpoint.

PUBLISHER: Explain that.

AUTHOR: I'll do so with a modern example. In 1951 Iran was ruled by a hereditary king called the Shah whose elected prime minister was Dr Mossadegh. Iranian oil then, as now, belonged to a private company with British and American shareholders. Dr Mossadegh's government nationalized the oil wells for the good of the Iranian people. Two years later a military group seized power and tried Mossadegh for crimes he had not committed, though news coverage in Britain and America described him as a thoroughly guilty man. The Shah became Iran's dictator and the original company got back the oil wells. Retired members of the British MI5 and American CIA have since boasted of how they funded and organized that coup – they view it as a discreet return of property to rightful owners. Having no shares in Anglo-Iranian Oil I think that company conspired with British and American governments to protect private wealth. I also think those who founded the United States, and United Irishmen, and British Friends of the People, and French National Assembly were early organizers of democracy, though except in Scotland their organizations were almost wholly middle class. Hereditary rulers viewed all such folk as conspirators against their property. Destroying infant democracies by underhand means was not practical then so monarchies made open war on them.

When the elected government of France was four years old Austria and Prussia invaded her threatening to "drown the Revolution in blood". France counter-attacked so strongly that by 1810 all west Europe except Britain and Spain were in a French empire where democracy was extinct. Napoleon was now an ally of the monarchs he had conquered, while making his brother king of Spain and south Italy. In Britain the House of Commons no longer wanted parliamentary reform because George III was now too insane to meddle with politics; also the war with France had brought the House of Commons all the middle-class support it needed – war with Napoleon was both popular and profitable. British fleets had destroyed the navies of France,

Denmark, Holland and Spain. They dominated every ocean and had secure ports on every coast, including the Mediterranean. A contemporary English satirist, Gillray, showed all this in a cartoon captioned *Leading Statesmen Enjoy a Little Supper*. The world lies like a plum pudding on a dish with little Napoleon on one side hacking off west Europe with his sabre; he is having trouble detaching Spain. Opposite him tall thin William Pitt, British prime minister, quietly removes most of the other continents.

The Society of United Irishmen was extinct. Helped by England the Protestant opposition grew too strong for it; the leaders had called in help from the French and been bloodily defeated. Ireland's parliament, like Scotland's ninety-three years earlier, had abolished itself in return for seats among the Westminster lords and commoners. This absentee Irish government was entirely Protestant, but it was thought that from London they could more easily manage the majority of Irish Catholics they did NOT represent. In both British islands the war was raising the price of corn and wool. Legislation was helping landowners evict small tenants and enclose commons, since new methods made it possible for them to cultivate more soil with fewer labourers – big profits for landlords! Many driven off the land found work in factories making weapons, boots, uniforms, other equipment for our armed forces and allies. Big profits for industry and trade!

At the start of the war factory owners had feared that able-bodied men joining the army would leave them too few workers and increase the price of labour. Prime minister Pitt advised them to get new machines which women and children could work. Costs would be further reduced by getting children from orphanages, housing them in sheds attached to the factories and paying them with food. This system greatly boosted Britain's industrial revolution and flourishes in south America and Asia to the present day.

In 1812 the handloom weavers found their employers' use of the system was forcing their wages down to starvation level, so they petitioned parliament to enforce a minimum rate of pay. The petition was rejected because the weavers were breaking a recent law against workmen combining to improve their condition. In Nottingham, Yorkshire and Lancashire weavers reacted by breaking into factories and wrecking the machines, but they calmed down when seventeen of them were arrested, tried, condemned, hung. But Scottish weavers found a legal redress not available in England.

A Scottish law empowered magistrates to fix a fair rate of pay in time of hardship. Glasgow weavers brought their case before magistrates who accepted the appeal, so employers took the case to Scotland's supreme court, the Court of Session. This court also decided that the weavers' claim was just, so employers ignored that decision. The weavers called a strike and at once magistrates who would not enforce the Scottish law on fair wages enforced the English law against workmen combining to get them. A weavers' meeting was fired upon by the military, six were killed, others arrested and charged with conspiracy and treason. Meanwhile the Scottish fair wages law was repealed in Westminster with the backing of the Scots MPs.

PUBLISHER: This is grim stuff!

AUTHOR: Yes. The Waterloo victory did not improve things though middle-class folk thought parliamentary reform could now be resumed. They organized a legally permitted reform meeting in a field called St Peter's near Manchester. Women and children attended with so many of the working class that the numbers grew to more than fifty thousand. It was a peaceful meeting but the size terrified local magistrates who dispersed it with mounted soldiers using sabres. Nine men, two women were killed, over five hundred folk wounded.

The government acted as promptly as after the small 1968 massacre in Derry. Magistrates and army were cleared of blame. Acts were passed making it treason to urge political reform; justices of the peace could order arrests and search of private property on suspicion; meetings of over fifty people were declared illegal; newspapers were made too dear to be bought by the working classes. This incident was called the Peterloo Massacre because it made many Britons feel as crushed as they thought the French felt after Waterloo. Having taken such strong steps the cabinet wanted the middle classes to see that an impending revolution made them necessary. With the help of a Scottish MP, a Glasgow businessman, some spies and a great deal of bribery the government achieved the great Scottish Insurrection of 1820.

It was timed to coincide with a genuine strike when all over Britain many workers did stay away from their factories. In two isolated weaving communities fraudulent posters and emissaries in government pay persuaded some weavers that all Scotland was in revolt. With clumsy weapons they marched out to join their comrades. All forty-seven were seized by expectant troops and and tried for treason. Most were sent to Botany Bay; Baird, Hardie and Purley Wilson were hung. Once more law and order had triumphed!

PUBLISHER: Why harp on all this out-of-date injustice?

AUTHOR: It is not out-of-date in a Britain whose present government (January 1997) denies a legal minimum wage to British workers because it will stem the profits of the wealthy. Nor are government spies, agent provocateurs and dirty tricksters things of the past. Their offices are in a splendid post-modernist structure on the opposite side of the Thames from Westminster Palace. This ministry of untruth, built and maintained at the taxpayers' expense, makes the Victorian-Gothic pile housing our government look comparatively quaint and toylike, but blends splendidly with the towers of adjacent international oil companies.

10
QUACKOCRACY

or,
From Waterloo to Sarajevo

BRITAIN HAD THE WORLD'S foremost political economists during the wars with France. None foresaw unemployment following victory, perhaps because Adam Smith never mentioned such a thing in *The Wealth of Nations.* Tens of thousands discharged from war-supply industries were joined by similar numbers of demobilized soldiers: hunger, desperate misery and riots ensued. Yet Britain now had the richest ruling class and biggest empire in the world! – she used Australia as the Russian Czars used Siberia, as a cheap gaol for thieves, poachers and political dissidents. The new situation needed new measures which Britain could afford – France's revolution had erupted during efforts to reform a bankrupt nation, not a wealthy one. The government set up a committee to collect advice on curing Britain's discontents without changing her six-centuries-old electoral system.

At first the committee was impressed by the advice of Robert Owen, owner and manager of New Lanark, a small Scottish industrial town he had partly created. He advised the government to make all British industries do what he had done: use profits above five per cent to improve living conditions and education of their workers, and to keep them employed at a basic rate when trade was slack. This policy (which the Japanese used to remake their nation after 1945) appealed to Tories whose main wealth was in agriculture, but political economists explained the scheme was Utopian because *the more prosperity you give the poor the more they will breed*. In other words, if an employing class abolishes poverty *now*, a generation hence its children will once more have to grapple with the surplus children of *their* employees. The prosperous should therefore keep their wealth and let unemployment, hunger and homelessness reduce the numbers of poor who can do very little damage to a strong nation where at least three quarters of the people are comfortable. Meanwhile a reservoir of unemployed strengthens industry by keeping down wages.

What Britain needed (said the economists who our rulers heeded) were military barracks near every large industrial city, a strong police force, huge new gaols (because the cost of shipping criminals to the far side of the globe was great and death for petty crimes was becoming unpopular); also institutions for the destitute where children were split from parents and husbands from wives – places so grim that paupers with a spark of self-respect spent their last few pennies on cheap gin and died of exposure in gutters rather than enter them. But unemployed or discontented workmen should be helped to emigrate, to Canada or other British colonies, partly through private charities, sometimes with government help.

Britain got these things. When the owner of a Scottish island decided to evict ALL his tenants a private charity paid for the vessel taking them over the Atlantic, British soldiers forced unwilling tenants onto it, while helping the demolition of dwellings so the natives could have nothing to return to.

PUBLISHER: That MUST have been an exceptional case!

AUTHOR: Not in Gaeldom. Irish rural evictions were

often helped by the army and mainland Britain paid no attention. The London *Times* sometimes reported highland evictions but Scottish papers ignored them because the owners were friends of the landlords.

PUBLISHER: I'm sure equally vile things were happening in other countries!

AUTHOR: (soothingly) Yes yes. And from now on I will speak of pleasanter things, starting with the Reform Bill of 1832 which progressive Britons had sought sixty years earlier.

Constituencies were redrawn to include every inhabited part of Britain. All men with a home valued at ten pounds a year were enfranchised, so company shareholders could vote but not factory workers, substantial farmers but not labourers, officers but not lower ranks. English voters were now roughly one in thirty adult males instead of one in fifty: Scottish voters were roughly one in fifty because though her population was a sixth of England and Wales she had only a tenth of MPs. Even so the reforms proved Scotland and England had very different political complexions. Before 1832 Scotland's less than five thousand voters returned nobody but Tories. Afterward over sixty thousand voters steadily returned a big Liberal majority until 1918. A great part of the English middle class voted Tory because they trusted their hereditary bosses – the Scots did not.

PUBLISHER: So some people were happier?

AUTHOR: But all who wanted democracy felt cheated. Thomas Carlyle voiced their frustration in his *French Revolution* published in 1837. Like all histories (especially this one) it evoked the past to explain the present. Carlyle described the first elected deputies of the French people marching to Notre Dame Cathedral for a thanksgiving service, Mirabeau, Danton and Robespierre among them, then says to his readers:

> *Yes, friends, ye may sit and look; bodily or in thought, all France, and all Europe may sit and look: for it is a day like few others. It is the baptism day of Democracy. A superannuated System of Society is now to die; and so, with death-throes and birth-throes, a new one is to be born. What a work, O Earth and Heavens, what a work! Battles and bloodshed, September Massacres, retreats of Moscow, Waterloos, Peterloos, Tenpound Franchises, Tarbarrels and Guillotines; and from this present date some two centuries of it still to fight! Two centuries; hardly less; before Democracy go through its baleful stages of* Quack*ocracy; and a pestilential World be burnt up, and have begun to grow green and young again.*

That prophecy cheers me. If true then democracy will dawn in AD 2037 and I will see it if I live to be a hundred and three.

In the nineteenth century Britain became the world's leading industrial supplier. The government's policy (said one prime minister) was to help the British buy cheap and sell dear in every market, so Britain occupied useful bits of China, policed the coasts of less civilized lands with gunboats, diddled France and Egypt out of the Suez Canal. The British army did badly when invading Russia in 1854 and South Africa in 1899, but British discipline, science and manufacture defeated people with less modern technologies. "This will give Christian troops a splendid advantage over the heathen," said the founder of Rhodesia to the British press when testing a new machine gun at Woolwich Arsenal.

Many Scots used imperial connections as ladders to careers elsewhere, others found profitable work at home. Industrial towns were built to extract deposits of coal, iron and shale-oil from the valley between Forth and Clyde. Those driven from western highlands and Ireland by evictions and famine enlarged the lowland workforce. Glasgow, fed by a Scottish steel industry, made ships, guns, railway locomotives so successfully that for a decade she was one of the world's richest cities beside London, Paris, Berlin, New York, Chicago. Aberdeen prospered through railways which let her supply England with fish from the North Sea, meat from east-coast farmlands. Edinburgh was still Scotland's legal capital and a centre of modern medical training. Though not a source of wealth for natives the highlands were fashionable because cabinet ministers killed stags, grouse and salmon there; the widowed queen spent half her time at Balmoral.

This vitality hid the fact that, except at local level, Scotland had no government. Ireland's MPs made her the most debated colony Britannia possessed but Scots MPs obeyed Tory or Liberal whips and voted as their leaders told them to. Scots who wanted better representation formed a Society for the Vindication of Scotland's Rights, a pressure group which tried to get the terms of the Treaty of Union obeyed – from government reports they proved the terms were still being broken to Scotland's disadvantage. British troops evicted highland tenants in ways which the London *Times* said would be impossible in England. Government grants went to police forces and poor relief in England and Ireland but not Scotland. Parliament had used the funds of an extinct Orkney bishopric to pay for London municipal lighting. This and much more had been done with the compliance of Scots MPs. Only one member for Edinburgh kept trying to discuss the effect of English legislation on Scotland. He was mockingly nicknamed "the MP for Scotland" and ignored as a bore by English members who knew the other Scots MPs had the same interests as themselves.

The MPs dealt with the evidence of the Scottish Rights campaign by boldly ignoring it. They could do so because only the labouring classes who did not vote felt deprived of their rights. Scotland's middle class thought themselves junior partners in a world-wide everlasting English Empire.

PUBLISHER: Please! BRITISH Empire!

AUTHOR: Yes Wales and Ireland and Scotland were in it but England's governing class led the way – insisted on leading the way – led so successfully that the Scottish middle class followed like sheep. Scottish education was Anglicized to make the bright students agreeable to bosses trained in those private boarding schools the English mysteriously call *public*. Gaelic was banned as a language, even in primary schools. Imagine how English five-year-olds would feel in a school where German teachers punished them for not talking German. German governments did force such teaching on parts of Denmark and France they conquered. The Scottish Education Department did it to the Gaels.

PUBLISHER: That was cruel, but would it not have been more cruel to leave them ignorant of English?

AUTHOR: Of course they should have been taught English – every child should learn a second language and the earlier they learn it the easier. Good schooling promotes self-confidence by enlarging on our parents' culture, not by denying it. This schooling aimed to replace Scottish culture with what would get high marks

in English civil service exams. It promoted obedience instead of self-confidence, memory instead of thought.
PUBLISHER: Surely that was also done by the state education system in England!
AUTHOR: Exactly. Scotland was conforming to a system designed to produce the lower ranks needed by English *public* school officers. Well, it helped us fight two world wars as fiercely as Germans who had also been trained to obey. The Anglicizing was never total. Good teachers could still foster intelligence here. Scottish working people still expected more from education than their southern equivalents, and sometimes got it. Yet the notion that schools should mainly teach obedience was revived in January 1997 by a cabinet minister who wants military exercises on the curriculum of state schools.
PUBLISHER: I'm glad you're getting closer to the twentieth century but you haven't talked us out of the nineteenth.
AUTHOR: British politicians want us back into it.

At the end of the nineteenth century poor students no longer came to Scottish universities with a sack of oats to feed them through the term, yet that tradition was still proudly referred to. The millionaire Andrew Carnegie gave Glasgow University some scholarships for students whose parents could not afford fees. The principal accepted them reluctantly because (he said) such charity insulted the Scots tradition of manly independence. He knew that the fees of nearly all his students were now paid by parents who could easily afford them, so must have thought that was also part of the Scottish independent tradition – in England people thought it just standard practice and had no moral objections to scholarships. Maybe the principal did not know John Knox had proposed state scholarships for the poor three and a half centuries before.

This harking back to a Scottish past which they hardly understood was frequent among our professional classes. They subscribed to huge monuments commemorating William Wallace, Burns, Walter Scott and Scottish regiments who, since 1707, had defended the United Kingdom all over the world. Hundreds of Burns clubs were formed, thousands of Burns suppers eaten, and though Burns had been a democrat who admired the French Revolution and Tom Paine's *Rights of Man* these feasts mostly celebrated a non-political and therefore sham form of Scottish brotherhood. (Women were excluded.) Scottish independence could only revive among those who wanted it because they most painfully lacked it: the labouring classes. Ireland showed the way.

In Ireland Michael Davitt, a Catholic Socialist, formed a league of small tenant farmers and villagers who began to resist eviction, withhold unfair rents and boycott landlords who tried to enforce them. Irish MPs led by Parnell gave political support. On the Isle of Skye some crofters followed that example. When Lord MacDonald deprived it of pasture the folk refused to pay rent and refused to obey an eviction order. Led by the women (who fought most vigorously for their homes) they first drove off the local policemen, then a detachment of police sent from Glasgow. The crofters won that battle (called the Battle of the Braes) because by 1882 the use of troops against British natives would lose the government votes. When nearly a thousand crofters and their supporters tried to occupy a sheep run on the island of Lewis they were driven off by soldiers brought by a gunboat, HMS *Jackal*, but the aims of the land-agitators were supported by both Irish MPs and by Gladstone, the Liberal leader, who made speeches against inherited privilege. He was knocked off that high moral pedestal for a while by the Tory prime minister Disraeli, who suddenly gave Britain what working-class movements had been demanding for over half a century – a vote for every registered male adult, regardless of income. This new reform bill allowed the immediate creation of a party not dominated by the wealthy – the first independent Scottish party in Westminster.

By a huge majority the highlands and islands took four seats away from the Liberals and gave them to the Crofters' Party, which promised to limit feudal laws letting landlords raise rents and evict. Gladstone needed the help of this party as much as the Tories needed the Ulster Unionists in 1996. An act was passed giving crofters the security they needed. In 1886 a majority of Liberal and Irish and Crofting MPs also helped Gladstone put into the statute book an act giving independent governments to Ireland, Scotland and Wales – meaning that the Liberal Party would create a United States of Britain when it had time. Alas, it never found the time because Britain was rotten with imperialists. To stop Ireland getting independence a number of Liberal MPs seceded and voted with Tories on imperial matters. This alliance kept the Tory Party in power for the next twenty years and led Britain into a territorial war against a small republic of Dutch farmers who knew how to use rifles. Like the Americans in Vietnam the British found outright victory impossible, though they herded women and children into the world's first civilian concentration camps where many died of diseases caused by bad sanitation and nourishment. The Boer War ended in 1902, the year Edward VII got crowned in Westminster with a choir singing a hymn to Britannia:

Wider still and wider
Shall thy bounds be set,
God who made thee mighty
Make thee mightier yet!

The tune resembled that of *Deutschland über alles*. So did the sentiment which made Britain's government clutch Ireland until most of the Irish voted for Sinn Feiners who went to gaol rather than enter Westminster.

In 1911 the last Liberal government to hold office had Winston Churchill for home secretary. The Unionists and Tories made it hard for him to give Ireland home rule but he wanted his party to keep its promise to the Scots and said that a Scottish parliament would cause "a great enrichment of the national life of Scotland, the political and public life of the United Kingdom". He said he was ready to push through the required legislation. He was quickly shifted to the admiralty where Asquith, the prime minister, felt Winston's impetuosity would be more useful. The long expected war with Germany now looked unavoidable.

11
INTO LIVING MEMORY

THOUGH RULERS of eighteenth-century Britain made occasional remarks about "the swinish multitude" they knew they were the same kind of animal as their underlings. Cabinet ministers lost fortunes in gambling clubs, swapped wives and mistresses, drank till they vomited. They also took it for granted that less wealthy folk with similar tastes would indulge them as far as their means allowed. They knew over-indulgence impoverishes people in every walk of life but did not think poverty itself a proof of moral or mental inferiority. In a popular comedy written six years before the French Revolution the hero, a low-bred barber, tells a great nobleman, "I have used more intelligence getting money for food to eat – just to eat! – than you have needed to govern a province for a year."

This easy going attitude to poverty was less possible in the nineteenth century because poverty took frightening new forms in slums spreading around profitable new industries. Those who profited preferred blaming the filthy houses, diseases and high infant mortality there upon the stupidity and viciousness of the workers, not upon low wages and frequent unemployment. Tories who made money out of land were usually the ones who passed laws forbidding factory work to children under nine, preventing children over nine from working more than twelve hours a day, and other legislation which Liberals denounced as state interference with the *natural* laws of supply and demand. At the end of the century medical records proved that the average height of private soldiers applying to join the army was much less than those who enrolled for earlier wars, especially in cities where twenty-eight per cent of applicants had defects caused by malnutrition. Such facts induced the last Liberal government to national insurance, labour exchanges and the dole. For a while the trade unions hoped the Liberal Party would represent them in parliament. The unions lost that hope soon after the First World War and Scotland, which had returned a steady Liberal majority since 1832, began returning a steady Labour majority.

HARDIE, Keir (1856–1915)

Labour leader. An illegitimate child who was compelled to work from the age of eight and was employed in mining from the age of 10, Hardie was victimized for his attempts to organize the Scottish coalfields. He studied at night school, gave up mining, became a journalist, contested the Mid-Lanark parliamentary seat (1888), and was returned for West Ham South (1892–5) and for Merthyr (1900–15). Founder-editor of the influential Labour Leader *(1889) and creator of the Independent Labour Party (1893), he was instrumental in the formation of the Labour Representation Committee in 1900 and became chairman and leader of the Parliamentary Labour Party in 1906. Trade Unionist, evangelical, pacifist, internationalist, vigorous supporter of the cause of women's suffrage, and Christian and temperance reformer, though he never himself held public office, he identified the Labour Party with a pragmatic form of socialism that, in due course, made it the principal alternative to the Conservative Party.*

Like all brief biographies of Hardie that extract from Collins' and Brown's excellent *Companion to British History* fails to mention that Hardie was also a member of the Scottish Home Rule Association. So were all the Scottish makers of the Labour movement, including Ramsay MacDonald, Britain's first Labour prime minister. These folk, together with James Connolly and working-class makers of the Irish republic, believed small self-governing nations were as essential to democracy as socialism.

PUBLISHER: You'd better not mention socialism – it's completely discredited nowadays. Most folk don't even know what it is. Do you know what it is?

AUTHOR: I know what the Labour Party once thought it was – a democracy where all essential services and industries were under the direct control of elected local and national government; a democracy without paupers and millionaires where the quality of our health care, education and legal justice would not vary with wealth privately inherited or accumulated.

PUBLISHER: It sounds like Utopia – or what the USSR claimed to be before it collapsed.

AUTHOR: Russian communism had nothing to do with what the old Labour Party attempted and partly achieved, though Conservatives refuse to believe it. The Labour Party in Britain was parliamentary from the start. It was not made by one man – many social and political groups combined to form it, and I will use family reminiscences to explain them. This will also explain my feelings about the *New* Labour Party. They are the feelings of someone whose kindly grandfather once protected his family from being bullied by rich neighbours next door, and now sees him capering at a party on the neighbours' lawn, waving his arms in the air and grinning insanely.

My father's father was a blacksmith in east Glasgow at the end of the last century; a deeply religious man of mild temper who never earned more than fifty shillings a week in his life. After forty years' work with the same firm he was told to get lighter work elsewhere and dismissed on the spot. The only work he could get was heavier, less skilled and less well paid as a heavy labourer, but he was not a crushed and embittered man. He assisted in the creation of Dalmarnock Road Congregational Church, giving it ten years' unpaid service as a cleaner because he could not give it money. He taught in the Sunday school and conducted services when the clergyman was ill. William Gladstone and Keir Hardie were his political heroes – Hardie had been invited to preach a lay sermon in his church, because Hardie was a Christian who believed Christ could only be served by serving our fellow men. Evangelical Christianity was a strong element in the making of the Labour Party, especially among the working classes.

My mother's father, Harry Fleming, was foreman in a Northampton shoe factory which fired him for being a trade unionist. His name was put on a blacklist which meant he could get no work in England, so he came with his wife and family to Glasgow – which proves that in those days Scottish and English employers had different blacklists. (Nowadays the Economic League has one blacklist for all Britain, and four years ago I was pleased to hear from a *Daily Record* journalist that my name was on it.) The Scottish Trade Union Congress was founded in 1897 and its English equivalent soon after. Both supported Labour Party candidates to represent them, but eventually agreed to put money into the Labour Party itself. Conservative commentators keep finding something sinister in this, and nothing sinister at all in their own party being financially supported by all sorts of big businesses. Before 1914 the Tory Party was financed by great inherited fortunes, the Liberals by business contributions and the sale of honours, the Labour Party from the funds of skilled labourers. The name *Labour Party* was deliberately chosen because this was not to be a party of the wealthy and fashionable.

Yet many wealthy, professional people supported the Labour Party, people who thought everyone should have the fair play which the English class system denied to the majority.

PUBLISHER: British class system!

AUTHOR: I prefer to call it English because Scots who thrived by it had been to Oxford and Cambridge. I admit that so did others who rebelled against it. The most effective of these rebels joined the Fabian Society. Fabians thought socialism would be gradually gained by more legislation of a sort which was already effective. Bernard Shaw, the best Fabian spokesman, told Glasgow audiences that they already lived in a state which was halfway to Communism. Their communal water supply was the finest in Britain. They had good drains, streets, public lighting, transport, wash-houses, parks, museums, libraries, schools, municipal vegetable and fish and meat markets, abattoirs, docks and police force, all created and maintained at public expense because private businesses could not be trusted with such essential services. The task was now to replace slums with good public housing before taking monopolistic businesses into public ownership via government control. That is how Fabians thought. Lawyers and civil servants among them advised politicians of any party who were legislating to make life fairer for people. Gavin Brown Clark, Crofters' MP for Caithness was a Fabian,

and founder of the Scottish Home Rule Association: also founder of Labour parties on both sides of the border.
PUBLISHER: Why does this history of the early Labour Party help your argument for Scottish Home Rule?
AUTHOR: Because the Labour Party was created by people who wanted Scottish self-government! I want to show how the party dropped the idea, and how a third generation Labour voter (me) has been forced back to it.

In 1914 Britain declared war because in trade and territory the German empire rivalled its own. The official reason was an 1839 treaty by which Britain and Germany guaranteed Belgian independence, and which Germany violated by going through Belgium to attack France. So Britain went to war "to preserve" – said the popular press – "the independence of small nations" – and Irish independence was shelved once again. Both sides expected to win by a swift crushing blow. In a few weeks the front lines of both empires interlocked across France and jostled bloodily against each other for four more years. The battles killed a higher proportion of Scots than English for three reasons which operate in every British war:

1 Scotland has always a higher peacetime rate of unemployment and emigration which warfare draws upon.
2 Scotland has a higher proportion of the working class than England so a higher proportion of men enter infantry regiments, the regiments in which most soldiers are killed.
3 Highland regiments have a tradition of being good at reckless charges, so when available British commanders put them first.

None of these reasons cast doubt on English courage or undervalue English losses, which in working-class districts were as bad as anything Scotland sustained, but despite the desperate efforts of Keir Hardie to get a way of ending this horrible war discussed in parliament it was never discussed. Lloyd George, the prime minister, announced war aims through the press without consulting parliament: Britain was fighting this war to end all wars, to make a land fit for heroes to live in, to hang the Kaiser, to make Germany pay. These were not aims which allowed peace with Germany to be negotiated. The more millions of men died the less politicians who had started the killing could admit *both* sides were part of a hellish accident – the only solution they could imagine was the absolute defeat of the other side by as many more deaths as were needed.

There was a bright side. British industry had been in a depression before the war; now it was booming from government contracts. Munition work gave so many civilians higher incomes that Glasgow landlords felt able to raise their rents. This provoked the first act of Scottish Home Rule to be accepted by a British government since the Battle of the Braes, and it too was begun by women. Housewives whose husbands were fighting or wounded were hit hardest. Those who could pay the greater rent struck in sympathy with those threatened with eviction because they could not. Lawyers in the Independent Labour Party defended them. So did the Clydeside Workers' Committee, which had been set up to negotiate better wages for the workers than the trade unions dared. The government responded with an act restricting British rents to pre-war levels.

My father joined the army in 1914, leaving it four years later with a stomach wound which brought him a small government pension. He missed the post-war unemployment which rose to twenty per cent on Clydeside by operating a cutting machine in a cardboard-box making factory until World War II. He told me of the public jubilation and excitement in Glasgow after the 1922 general election which returned the first Labour Party majority in history. Ten Clydeside MPs were returned by the Scottish Independent Labour Party, a more socialist party than its English equivalent. Some of them, after denouncing the creation of private fortunes out of war industries, had been gaoled for pacifism or sedition. Services of dedication and thanksgiving were held in Glasgow City Hall and St Andrew's Hall. From local Labour branches all over the city processions converged to see the new MPs off to Westminster. Newspapers claimed that roughly a quarter of a million people brought traffic to a halt by filling Argyle Street, Buchanan Street and other approaches to St Enoch's Station. From the top of the ramp leading to it (now the approach to St Enoch's shopping mall) a former engineering shop-steward called David Kirkwood told the people, "When we return the railway will belong to us!" – meaning it would be nationalized. The crowd sang *Scots Wha Hae*, *A Man's a Man for a' that*, Blake's *Jerusalem*, *The Red Flag* and the *Internationale*.

The millennial mood came partly from socialists like my father whose educations made them think the election of a people's government was foretold by Christ when he said the lowly would be lifted up, the meek would inherit the earth. Since most Clydeside Catholics were of Irish extraction they had voted Labour because that party supported Irish independence, and the other parties had just torn Ireland in two, welding the industrial part into the British empire by giving it a separate parliament in Belfast, but radical Catholics had also formed Socialist societies. Many Protestants had voted Labour because they believed Labour victory was the final triumph of a struggle they had inherited from William Wallace, the Covenanters, radical weavers, Chartists' Co-operative Societies and socialist Sunday schools. Another element in the enthusiasm of the crowd may have been women, because for the first time *women of thirty and over* had been granted the vote. Parliament had decided they deserved it because they had worked so patriotically during the war, but the Labour Party promised them electoral equality with men.

This unity of political and religious faith may seem ridiculous to some readers. I cannot think of it without tears. These Clydesiders who the Fabians described as extremists entered Westminster (says one commentator) "burning with indignation at the social evils around them and missionary in their zeal to correct them". But the new Labour government was too weak to do anything without Liberal or Tory support, and organized against it were the banks and businesses and big landowners, also the Monarchy and House of Lords and Established Churches, three huge blockages to democracy which the Americans had shrugged off in the eighteenth century and the French (after five revolutions) in the nineteenth, but which the English ruling class (which knows how to make history serve it) maintains to this moment of writing – 6.17 p.m., Wednesday the fourth of February 1997.

PUBLISHER: I'm glad you've noticed the time. May I remind you that this pamphlet won't be printed in time for the next election if you don't finish writing it the day after tomorrow?

AUTHOR: Please don't interrupt! I'm bringing the past

up to date as fast as I can and there are precious details I MUST not omit.

In the 1920s three acute thinkers believed the Scottish Independent Labour Party's attempt to make Britain socialist by going to Westminster was as futile as the Scottish Presbyterians' attempt to make Britain Presbyterian by going there in Cromwell's time. These thinkers are dismissed as eccentrics by Scots who find most of their culture eccentric because they view it from an English home-counties standpoint. Welsh and north English folk may not find them so odd because they too have had such thinkers.

1 Guy Aldred was an English anarchist who settled in Glasgow because despite being gaoled again and again for anti-government speeches he found Glasgow congenial. He said Scottish socialist MPs should stay in Scotland as the Irish had done and make their own government.

2 John Maclean was a Marxist schoolteacher dismissed by Glasgow Education Department for supporting the housewives' rent strike in 1915. He thought that people who worked the land, mines and factories should take them over and operate them for the sake of each other, not for the profit of shareholders. He knew such takeovers would be difficult because the monetary system and established governments were controlled by such shareholders who also controlled the army and police. Only a politically educated working class could carry through the revolution he wanted so he founded the Scottish Labour College and travelled the country holding classes which recruited many working men. After the Soviet Revolution Lenin made him the Russian government's only British consul – nobody in England wanted the job

because the British government refused to recognize the post-Czarist government, and put an army on Russian soil to fight an undeclared war against it. Yet Maclean refused to join the Communist Party of Great Britain because he saw it would be a tool of Russian foreign policy and said Scotland should never be ruled from Moscow. He died aged thirty-four, his health broken by six arrests on charges of sedition and incitement to strike followed by spells in Edinburgh's Calton gaol, demolished now, but then a very tough gaol indeed. The regime was mainly solitary confinement with a diet of water, bread, porridge and occasional soup. Political prisoners who had been there needed medical treatment to recover afterwards.

3 Hugh MacDiarmid was the son of a postman in a border weaving town – became a journalist and Labour councillor in an east-coast fishing port – became Scotland's greatest poet since the death of Burns. He also founded the National Party of Scotland in 1928, because it was then clear that the Labour Party would not keep its promises to give Scotland home rule: the more socialist of the English MPs needed Scottish help and Scots MPs wanted to give it. MacDiarmid declared that in Westminster and out of it most Scots had opted for cosy mediocrity by running their country as an English province. He also said that small independent nations needed international outlooks, and found his in the Communist Party of Great Britain which Maclean had rejected. MacDiarmid was later expelled from the National Party of Scotland for his communism and from the Communist Party for his nationalism. He said:

I mon aye be whaur extremes meet –
It is the only way I ken
To dodge the curst conceit of being right
That damns the vast majority of men.

This man was not suited for party politics, yet the party he helped to create (after some splits and rejoinings of a sort which once afflicted the Scottish Kirk) has now three seats in Westminster, had 11 seats in 1974, and will have many more in future if Tony Blair does not give Scotland some kind of parliament after the next election. The Scottish National Party also promises that its MPs will stay in Scotland as soon as the Scots vote in a majority of them.

I admire and sympathize with the three great dissenters listed above but cannot share their view of the Clydeside MPs and old parliamentary Labour Party. They did me and my family and our neighbours and nearly all my friends so much good that I am as grateful to them as any Etonian or Oxonian to the founders of *his* institutions. This extract from *The People's Dictionary of Caledonian Worthies* partly explains why.

WHEATLEY, *John (1869–1930)*

Born in County Waterford he was brought as an infant to Baillieston, near Glasgow. Here he worked in a coalmine from the age of 12 to 24, then in his brother's grocery shop, then as a journalist who became partner in a printing firm. In 1906 he founded the Catholic Socialist Society which got him denounced by the local hierarchy which had not then reached its unofficial concordat with the Glasgow Labour Party. He had been one of eight children living with parents and sometimes a lodger in a one-room flat without piped water or lavatory, so wanted good housing for everyone. A leading "Red Clydesider", in 1924 he was made housing minister in the first Labour government and achieved one of its few successes: he introduced generous state support for municipal house building. The Wheatley Acts (as they were called) quickly changed the appearance of towns throughout Britain.

12 DEMOCRACY: BRITISH DAWN & ECLIPSE

BEFORE 1939 BRITISH WARS were declared by confident politicians who saw something to be gained by them. Most people gained nothing from wars but employment during it and a slump afterward. Two slumps happened between 1918 and 1939. Both impoverished millions of wage earners, but the second also damaged stock-exchange speculators (who had caused it) and reduced the value of private investments. Bankers urged the government to cut expenditure on social welfare. A Labour government was in office but not in power because as usual the other MPs were too many for it. Most Labour MPs, especially the Clydesiders, rejected these cuts which would make the poor poorer. Their leader, Ramsay MacDonald, decided to act without them. He united with Tory and Liberal leaders to make a new government called the National Government, called a general election and won the greatest electoral victory in British history – 554 seats (470 of them Tory) with only 46 Labour MPs in opposition.

PUBLISHER: Why tell us this?

AUTHOR: Ramsay MacDonald was not only the first Labour prime minister, he was also a Scottish Labour prime minister who rejected socialism, putting the good of money-marketers before the good of most wage earners. We may soon have another like him.

PUBLISHER: But the money-marketers *employ* the wage earners, or finance the firms that employ them, so the health of the money market comes first, whether you like it or not.
AUTHOR: An English economist called Keynes urged another way of beating economic depression and an American president practised it. The government reduces unemployment and promotes industry by ordering public works – irrigation, forestation and building. Instead the National Government abolished municipal housing subsidies, and employed spies to seek reasons for cutting people's dole money. A huge army of unemployed marched to London – the hunger marchers – the Scottish Independent Labour MPs took the leaders to 10 Downing Street. For old times' sake the prime minister saw the MPs (their votes had put him in office) but he refused to see the hunger marchers. Poor MacDonald was now a complete Toom Tabard. The Tories soon replaced him with one of their own, Stanley Baldwin. In 1938 a survey indicated that a third of the British people lived in a state of poverty which endangered their health and a third lived very near to that, but the National Government refused to tackle poverty until forced by Adolf Hitler.

Britain declared war on the Kaiser as soon as Germany violated Belgian neutrality. Hitler's forces entered the Rhineland, bombed Spanish civilians, annexed Austria, occupied Czechoslovakia before a British prime minister asked him to stop doing these things. Britain was terrified of entering another world war: the Labour Party was partly pacifist, many Tories thought Hitler an ally against Russian communism, even British communists thought Hitler an ally when he joined Stalin to dismember Poland. The British prime minister who declared war in 1939 was not a confident man asserting imperial prestige but a worried man who felt threatened by a megalomaniac. In 1940 he was replaced by a prime minister who had annoyed the British for years by saying Hitler would have to be fought, had annoyed others in World War I by saying (though he was not a socialist) that a socialist economy was best for a government fighting a war. Most of Churchill's colleagues and advisers had fought in that war and agreed with him.

The Churchill government took direct control of land, food production, transport and industry. Labour Party people were put in charge of these because they knew best how they worked. Morrison, minister of supply, had organized the London transport system; Bevin, minister of labour, was a founder of trade unions – he directed all domestic servants under a certain age into war work. The government fixed profits, wages, prices and rents; banned private motoring for all but public servants (doctors were registered as public servants); rationed food and clothing so that only those who broke the law could get extra – and most Britons, even the wealthy, were law abiding. To unify war effort the coalition government used a degree of management beyond anything Hitler attempted, but Hitler's notion of government was infantile: he would enrich his followers by plundering all Jews inside Germany and all foreigners outside. British national unity was also helped by the London blitz. Centres of government and broadcasting were dispersed through the rest of Britain. Servicemen passing through the capital were not, as in World War I, offended by the sight of wealthy people revelling in luxurious entertainments. Through changes of employment caused by the war, and clothes rationing, and prevalence of uniforms, by 1944 it was almost impossible in Britain to tell someone's social origins by their mere appearance.

PUBLISHER: You are evoking a united Britain which runs directly against your argument.

AUTHOR: Not if you follow me to the end! The unity of wartime Britain made it a subject of nostalgic film-making and political rhetoric almost before it stopped, but few films and less rhetoric mention that the unity was got by measures previously rejected as socialism. As in World War I government propaganda promised the British people that they were fighting for a better Britain, and the Labour part of that government meant to prove that these promises would not be lies – that this war would not be followed by a slump, unemployment and the widespread poverty existing before it.

Keynes, the economist who thought unemployment curable, was now adviser to the treasury. With Beveridge, a former labour exchange director, he drafted a plan converting the old Liberal state insurance scheme into a welfare service giving EVERYONE some of the security enjoyed by those with large incomes, earned or unearned. It was an up-to-date version of the scheme proposed by Tom Paine in his *Rights of Man* in 1791, but less revolutionary. It would be funded by money drawn from everybody's income without disturbing the class divisions between monarch and charwoman – a compromise only the British could have conceived. In the first general election after the war a Labour Party was voted in by a huge majority because it promised to carry out this plan. It did. Britain's health services, coalmines, railways, gas and electricity supplies were speedily nationalized by amending for peace legislation which had used them for war. Ardent Labour voters (and though not yet fifteen in those days I was one of them in spirit) were proud of Britain because it had carried through a socialist revolution without injuring a soul. We were an example to the USA because our parliament ruled big businesses for the good of everyone, an example to Soviet Russia because our government was an elected parliament: not a self-perpetuating minority party which excluded all others.

It was only much later that I realized the British Labour revolution had done Britain's moneyed interest (as Jonathan Swift called it) more good than harm. The owners of British railways and coalmines were paid large compensation for shares in businesses which, between the wars, had become unsaleable except at a loss. Moreover, the class of people who had once owned the nationalized industries now drew fat salaries by sitting on the boards which administered them – retired admirals and military men were thought fit for such jobs, and peers of course, and folk with private business interests elsewhere. The state industries were now being managed by the class which destroyed and privatized them for its own advantage thirty years later. Why was not at least half the management of British Railways elected by railway workers? Because Britain is not managed that way. Yet throughout the fifties and sixties many wealthy folk kept hinting that a social revolution had destroyed a splendid civilization which was their heritage before World War II. The purest essence of this attitude is conveyed in *Brideshead Revisited*, a book I hated because the author's snobbery clashed with my own. I believed that Riddrie was a much higher level of civilization than the splendid estate of Brideshead.

Riddrie was a Glasgow housing scheme of three-storey tenements fronted with red sandstone and pebble-dashed semi-detached villas. The back green of the tenement where I grew up was carpeted with real green grass, and in our close lived a nurse, postman, printer who worked on the *Glasgow Herald*, the local tobacconist and my father, so I had no doubt that Riddrie contained people who were essential to human life – nowadays I am less sure. Food is the first essential. It is probable, however, that some of the wage-earners in Riddrie had a function in the Glasgow meat or fish or vegetable market. However, as in Brideshead, the people who presided were women because the men of the place went to work outside it. Everybody over middle age tends to romanticize their childhood, but I know Riddrie was one of the first housing estates built under the Wheatley Acts, and I am sure it was one of the best designed, with shops and primary school and municipal bowling green (where my English grandfather won a trophy) and allotments and public park. There was also a Protestant and a Catholic church, but my parents had not forced the burden of an immortal soul upon me, so to me the spiritual and mental power-house of Riddrie and also (when I was old enough to get political convictions) the pinnacle of socialist civilization was the public library, where I discovered William Blake and Heinrich Heine (in translation) and Hogg's *Confessions of a Justified Sinner* and Sartre and Thurber and more wonderful, influential people than I can list here. It was a source of wonder and gratitude to me that anybody could enter and browse through this warm quiet treasury of alternative worlds. I knew that like my healthcare and education and school milk and Glasgow Art Gallery this was paid for out of the earnings of grown-ups like my father, but I knew he approved of this social, sociable, socialist arrangement and I could imagine no more perfect one. I expected the world to become a mosaic of Riddries, each with a strong local flavour of course, when all civilization had taken the path which John Wheatley had laid down for British socialism.

PUBLISHER: Ingsoc.

AUTHOR: What?

PUBLISHER: In *Nineteen Eighty-Four* George Orwell called it English Socialism – Ingsoc.

AUTHOR: I was fourteen or fifteen when I read that book and it made me miserable for a fortnight – I've been unable to open it since. Ingsoc was the kind of one-party political state Orwell imagined spreading throughout the world after a short nuclear war. People who have lived inside the recently deceased Russian empire say it described the mentality of middle and upper classes there quite accurately, but it was not Ingsoc which made me want Scottish home rule, it was the Labour Party's increasing Toryism – its subservience to what Jonathan Swift called *the moneyed interest* which continually profits from warfare and preparations for warfare.

PUBLISHER: But five paragraphs ago you said World War II did not profit the British moneyed classes – that it persuaded them into something like a share-out.

AUTHOR: It did, but not into such a share-out that they lost their grip upon what someone once called the Commanding Heights of the Economy. During World War II an incident occurred which had also happened in World War I. An RAF bomber plane was returning from a German raid with bombs to spare when it occurred to the pilot that, by a very slight divergence from his flight path, he could drop these bombs on one of Krupp's armament factories, so he did so without having been ordered to. He was therefore court martialled for disobeying orders. The carefully contrived fire-storm which obliterated the civilian city of Dresden *could* have been used against Krupp's.

PUBLISHER: That was over half a century ago, and no sensible reader will trust an argument based on international conspiracies. Stick to your personal history.

AUTHOR: That's easy, because in my teens and twenties I thought the Labour Party had freed Britain from the pressures of international finance. Even Tory politicians had kept wartime promises to make Britain a better nation for everyone. Rab Butler, who was minister for education in Churchill's cabinet, introduced education grants enabling me and at least two generations of British children to get the college and university educations we were qualified for, though our parents would pay for them through their rates and taxes. In the fifties and sixties I took the future of British socialism for granted. My only dread was the atomic war which Britain, Russia and the USA were arming themselves to fight or (as the politicians who authorized the expense of it said) to prevent.

Most British Labour voters did not see why the USA, when she was the only nation to possess atomic weapons, refused to sign an international agreement banning their manufacture and use. Still less did we see why Britain (which now had no empire to defend) was joining an arms race with the two biggest empires which remained: especially when Japan and West Germany were becoming the world's foremost industrial nations because they were excluded from such weapon making. We could not understand it – there seemed no explanation but human blindness. Leading politicians in those days spoke as if nuclear war was a thing civilization could survive, while at the same time building vastly expensive bunkers for themselves and their

adherents all over the country. Bunkers for Scottish administrators were built under Edinburgh Zoo and the Glasgow Burrell Collection Gallery.
PUBLISHER: Thank goodness you've brought the topic back to Scotland. Were you converted to Scottish home rule by the placing of American and British nuclear submarine bases on the Clyde?
AUTHOR: No. I joined a political movement founded by four Englishman: Priestley the novelist, Russell the philosopher, Collins the priest and Foot the Labour politician. Since the British press is predominantly owned by Conservatives the CND campaigners were mocked as exhibitionists or denounced as agents of Russian foreign policy. We were told that without nuclear weapons Britain would become second rate like Japan, West Germany and Scandinavian nations where the ordinary standard of living had risen mysteriously higher than that of Britain. Despite this publicity our trade unions and local Labour parties were so convinced by CND arguments that the 1960 Labour Party conference voted that Britain give up her nuclear defences – whereupon the leader of the parliamentary Labour Party said he would ignore the conference's decision. In this matter he was on the side of the Tories, and the parliamentary Labour Party has been on the side of the Tories in that and other matters ever since.

At the time I was naively astonished. My schooling had taught me that the British two-party political system was best in the world because at each general election the voters would be offered two programmes to choose between. Inevitably the Tory programme would be to keep the greatest wealth and authority in the hands of those who already had it. Inevitably the opposition would provide an alternative programme to reduce established power for the benefit of the poorly paid, and the electorate would choose between them as they had done in 1945. AND NOW THE LEADER OF MPs PUT INTO PARLIAMENT BY TRADE UNIONS AND LOCAL LABOUR PARTIES WAS DENYING ITS ROOTS **IN ORDER TO DEPRIVE BRITISH VOTERS OF A CHOICE!** ***HOW COULD HE?***

PUBLISHER: Stop shouting.

AUTHOR: ***BUT HOW COULD HE?***

PUBLISHER: This emotionalism will repel Scottish voters and be derided by reviewers.

AUTHOR: But our Labour leaders are supporting the fucking *British nuclear* so-called *deterrent* to the present day! It proves that Britain is still the quackocracy Carlyle noticed in 1832!

PUBLISHER: I advise you to take a short walk, cool down and write what I hope is the last chapter.

AUTHOR: I will, after offering another extract from *The People's Dictionary of Caledonian Worthies.*

BOYD ORR, *John (1880–1971)*

Biologist. The son of an Ayrshire farmer, he took a medical degree at Glasgow University which opened his eyes to the combination of disease, hunger and poverty in city slums. He served with distinction in World War I winning the DSO and MC. In 1929 he founded the Imperial Bureau of Animal Nutrition in Aberdeenshire with government aid, and used it to promote his main interest which was the nutrition of human beings. Using evidence obtained with great difficulty from reluctant local governments he proved that in the poorest parts of Britain over twenty per cent of schoolchildren suffered from malnutrition, and persuaded the National Government to give them milk through their teachers. Churchill made him minister of health during the war, and he swiftly set up a system of medical inspection, cod liver oil and orange juice distribution: this resulted in the generation of children which grew up in World War II being the healthiest ever recorded when it ended. From 1945 to 48 he was the first director of the United Nations Food and Agricultural Organization. He attempted to set up a world food bank which would be used to fight famines in any nation where they occurred, but resigned in disgust when he discovered nations with food surpluses would only give them to poorer nations on terms which destroyed the receivers' national independence. His prophecies got him caricatured as a prophet of doom by the press; for his services in the aftermath of war he received the Nobel Peace Prize. Having decided that the only hope for small nations lay in cultivating their own resources, especially the food supply, he retired to a Scottish farm purchased for his son-in-law and became a supporter of the Scottish National Party.

13
THE UNLUCKIEST CHAPTER

THE POVERTY OF SCOTLAND was often referred to by eighteenth-century satirists who regretted the Act of Union. They said it explained why parliament was infested by Scottish sycophants supporting England's most reactionary political party. After 1832 the parliamentary Scots became steady supporters of the Liberal Party but more respectable. Most of their countrymen were poorer than the English but their land and industries were sources of wealth. After 1922 a Labour majority replaced the Liberal one as the poor state of Scottish heavy industries became obvious, and the boost these were given by World War II outlasted it by very few years. In 1969 and 70 the discovery of North Sea oil caused a flurry of hopefulness in Scotland but by 1974 it was obvious that whatever revenues Britain drew from oil were benefiting very little of Scotland outside Aberdeenshire. The cabinet minister overseeing the industry turned out to have large shares in it and was persuaded to retire, but without much protest from Labour the oil rights were leased to completely private companies – the Norwegian government kept a majority share in its North Sea oil wells.

Two general elections in 1974 raised the Scottish National Party MPs from one to seven and then eleven. In alliance with thirteen Liberals who also promised Scotland home rule they could influence a Labour government which ruled by a narrow majority. The government appointed a Royal Commission to report and advise on the state of Scotland and the Commission's report and advice confirmed every detail of the Scottish National Party's opinion: compared with England and other west European nations Scotland's state was very poor indeed. Life expectancy was lower, unemployment much higher. Industries were closing because capital was being drawn to the south. Once vital Scottish firms had become branches of international ones which tended to close them down. The cleverest Scots usually looked for jobs in other countries. The Commission advised that the best way to restore Scottish vitality was through its own elected parliament.

The Labour government had to accept the diagnosis of the disease but disagreed completely with the recommended cure, though having none of its own to offer. In this, of course, it was completely in agreement with the front bench of the Tory party. However, it agreed to let the people of Scotland vote on the matter, though by a last-minute amendment it declared that a majority in favour of home rule would only obtain that if it was forty per cent of the Scottish electorate – in other words, the fastest horse would lose the race unless it won by a head and neck. In the build-up to the referendum the Labour prime minister Mr Callaghan, the leader of her majesty's opposition Mr Heath, both told Scottish voters that an independent government for their nation would drive capital out of Scotland at an even faster rate, causing greater loss of industry and cuts in public services. As a result the Labour government put on the statute book an act giving Scotland home rule, just as the Liberal Party had done in 1886. But first the Scots had to vote on it.

In 1979 they were allowed to vote on the single issue

of their own government for the first time in history, and despite adverse publicity from most of the British media and nearly all Tory and Labour politicians who spoke on the matter, a majority of thirty-three per cent wanted it, thirty-one per cent rejected it, thirty-six per cent abstained from voting. The fastest horse lost the race because it had won by a short head. Those who wanted most of Scotland to reject independence could not pretend the result was a victory for them – they cast disdain on the Scots for "being unable to make their minds up".

PUBLISHER: Still, a two per cent lead wasn't much.

AUTHOR: In a recent Quebec referendum those against independence outvoted those for it by one per cent. The will of the majority was allowed to prevail. Democracy means that in several other lands, but not in our nation of parliamentary quacks.

PUBLISHER: Thirty-six per cent is a very high abstention rate.

AUTHOR: I can sympathize with it. Many people have no faith nowadays in any kind of parliament. But a Scottish one is our only chance of making a difference to ourselves.

May I remind you that everything we were told would happen if Scotland got her own parliament has happened without it? Our mining industry, car industry, steel industry have been run down like Clyde shipyards and Paisley textiles with the Fort William pulp mill and Invergordon aluminium works. These were all things a Scottish parliament would have had to oppose or seek to replace. Every good thing that Scotland and England had in common, all that made our nations good examples to others has been sold off or hideously cheapened. In twenty-five years the party that claims to support traditional values has dismantled an egalitarian educational system founded by John Knox and modernized by Rab Butler, public libraries and transport systems and water supplies created by nineteenth-century Liberals, the Wheatley housing schemes. Gambling used to be denounced as a vice of the working classes and idle rich. Now people are encouraged to support charities and community projects through a state-run lottery which puts the bets of the poor into the pockets of the wealthy.

It's a Wonderful Life is a film in which a good little businessman has helped his local community through some small-scale house purchase scheme, thus keeping many people out of the clutches of a wicked money lender. At a distressing moment in later life he wishes himself dead and is cured of the wish by being shown his home town as it would have been without him. It has become a garish Las Vegas glittering with adverts for strip shows and gambling, the streets full of conspicuously wealthy folk in flashy cars beside beggars and a prostitute in whom he recognizes the faces of old school friends and the girl next door – the values of the rich money lender have prevailed. That is how I feel about modern Britain.

This book, alas, is only half the work I meant it to be. With information supplied by Angel, Chris, May, Eleanor, Archie, Sonia, Tom and others in law, libraries, social work, nursing, doctoring, teaching, journalism, local politics. I had meant to create a mosaic of other people's words and experience bringing the past completely up to date. It would explain how and why big fortunes now get paid to folk for undoing things – promoting ignorance, beggary, homelessness, by closing nurseries, schools and hospitals – and for not doing things (example: the Governor of the Bank of England being paid over a million *not* to grow corn on his large private estate). It would show why the only industries enthusiastically promoted in England now are finance, weapons manufacture, advertising and spying. It would explain why the Labour Party has grown more right wing as the Tory party has grown more right wing, and why the Scottish Labour councils love Big Brother – co-operate more enthusiastically with Tory governments in Westminster than some English Conservative councils do. It explains why Britain is a worse country.

PUBLISHER: Many people don't feel that way. They feel the country is richer, more democratic, more prosperous since Margaret Thatcher destroyed the power of trade unions and local governments. What would you say to *them*?

AUTHOR: I suppose their prosperity has increased with privatization, homelessness, crime and parliamentary corruption, and that one of four simple faiths lets them feel satisfied.

1 *Most folk in Britain are not much worse so the rest can be ignored.*

This faith may be defunct as Tory cabinet ministers have publicly complained of increased crime and beggary.

2 *Life is made hard for many people by monetary forces not even economists understand, so we had better keep the present state of Britain until things improve.*

This is the faith of Allan Massie who, in a thoughtful pamphlet, referred to the "utterly mysterious nature of money". I think that remark naive. Money is not mysterious to bankers, brokers and financiers. They may miscalculate but are hardly ever impoverished. In recent years only one millionaire needed to commit suicide. The only one sent to jail for fraud was swiftly reprieved on grounds of ill health, and is now as fit and free as ever.

3 *Before 1979 the welfare state gave the working classes security and leisure by taxing their social superiors. This destroyed the family values of many workers and made their children and/or grandchildren unfit for honest work. The de-industrialization of Britain with increasing homelessness, crime etcetera has been caused by the large number of slackers who refuse to work for a place in our juster, harder social order.*

This is Margaret Thatcher's faith. I have heard it said by people like me whose parents or grandparents were working class, and who were helped into professional jobs by the welfare state. They now think it has served their purpose and should be dismantled. I cannot argue with them.

4 *A healthy money market needs docile work-forces. Feeble trade unions, a high level of poverty and unemployment ensure docility when assisted by police with almost unrestricted powers of arrest. Britain has all that now, besides a government which recognizes the supremacy of the money-market, so there's hardly anything wrong with modern Britain.*

Money lovers have preached this sort of faith in every age, liking to shock with what they call "realism". In the mid 19th century they said the potato blight had done very little good because it only killed a million Irish.

The 2nd of these faiths explains the policy of Labour governments between 1964 and 79, the last explains the legislation of Tory governments since. The legislation was passed to strengthen Britain's money market at the expense of all her other industries but arms making. Straight monetary rhetoric would have frightened many voters, so Mrs Thatcher was elected because she believed in the moralistic bletherings of faith number 3. The press loved her for it.

PUBLISHER: Do you think an independent Scotland could work without the international money markets?

AUTHOR: I know it couldn't. But I think it could emulate countries whose small local money markets support national communities without huge class difference, countries where public services are still efficient, crime and destitution are not taken for granted, national pride is shown without military display or pompous ceremonial. I mean the Scandinavian countries.

Two of these, Denmark and Finland, have nearly the same populations as Scotland – slightly more than five million. Norway and Iceland have 4.3 and a quarter million. Sweden, the biggest, has 8.6 million. The Scottish worker's standard is below that of the English because of lower wages and higher unemployment; but the English worker's standard of living is below that of the Scandinavian.

PUBLISHER: Surely these five countries are not equally wealthy?

AUTHOR: They can't be. Iceland is mostly uninhabited wilderness of lava and glacier – fish is the only export. Norway, mountainous and fjord-riven, has a coastal fringe of farming and fishing communities. The low-lying, thoroughly farmed Danish peninsula and islands form the smallest and most thickly peopled nation. Sweden and Finland are vastest, with greater variety of landscape than I can indicate in a sentence. With all their variety these five nations share a basis of social welfare which Britain has abandoned or perhaps never reached.

PROPOSED NORDIC UNION, CIRCA 2001AD

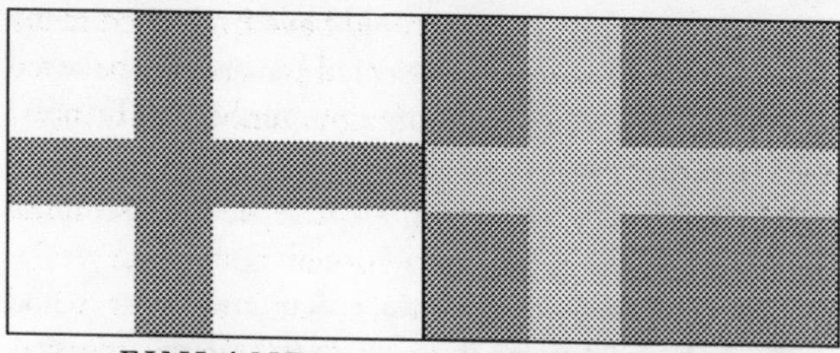

FINLAND
5 million folk – 131,000 sq. miles

SWEDEN
8.6 million folk – 159,000 sq. miles

SCOTLAND
5.1 million folk – 30,000 sq. miles

DENMARK
5.1 million folk – 17,000 sq. miles

NORWAY
4.3 million folk – 125,000 sq. miles

ICELAND
0.26 million folk – 40,000 sq. miles

From this I deduce that a nation's prosperity should not be judged by the number of millionaires who live there, or by the wealth of its financial houses, or by its capacity to poison the globe with sophisticated weapons. National prosperity happens where people share most equally the wealth of the goods their land produces, and this is most likely to happen in small democratic nations. The most recent example of small-nation prosperity is the Irish Republic, its economy now surpassing Britain's in growth and income per head.

PUBLISHER: The Irish Republic is in the European Community.

AUTHOR: And there, perhaps, is Scotland's best chance of independence under its own government: a government which can regard the government of England in London as a neighbour whose greater bulk and spending power has to be considered, but whose control over the life of Scotland is no greater than Spain's over the life of Portugal. True friendship is only possible between partners who are equally dependent on each other, or equally independent. The first option is impossible – England's population has been about nine times Scotland's for centuries. The second option is possible if we work for it.

PUBLISHER: Chapter 1 said the ground of your argument was Scottish geography. You've wandered from that.

AUTHOR: I'll return to it. Scotland is a cluster of islands, most of them not separated by water. This variety was held together by a government which suddenly, against the wishes of the people, became a fraction of a London assembly. Since then the Scots have been ruled by local bosses who take their orders from party managers in London: Tory from 1707 until 1832, Liberal from 1832 till 1922, Labour almost ever since. English outnumber Scots by nine to one, and as both lands vote differently Scottish politicians have made no difference to how Britain is governed since the 1920s. Scotland's strongest political party grew complacent with failing to promote its policies because England rejected these. It grew so complacent that it forgot its original policies – socialism and home rule.

No surprise was caused by a recent leader of Scotland's Labour Party Executive announcing he would rather oppose a permanent Tory government in London than be in the Labour government of independent Scotland.

PUBLISHER: But Tony Blair has committed his party to a separate Scottish assembly.

AUTHOR: Perhaps. It is likely to be what Billy Connolly calls a *pretendy* parliament: a big London firm's branch office where local complaints get stifled by the locally complacent. It will only be a step nearer democracy if Scots refuse to let it rest at that.

14
WELLBEING: A FICTION

which I hope is as unlike Scotland 2020 as England 1984 was unlike Orwell's tale.

I SAW A PLAIN strewn with marble rocks, the smallest higher than a man, the largest as big as a cathedral. They were pieces of a statue that had once stood taller than Ben Nevis. Groups of little people moved with horse-drawn wagons among these rocks. They were searching for one small enough to carry away yet recognizably human – the lobe of an ear or tip of a toe. Each group wanted to remove such a fragment to where they could love and pray to it, because it proved there had been power and beauty the world no longer contained. One group found a rock pierced by a beautifully smooth oval arch, part of a nostril. As they lifted it into their cart other groups combined to attack and rob them. This happened to all who found a good fragment, so none was ever carried away and love and prayer were impossible. I opened my eyes because my Japanese host was asking a question.

"In the second chapter of book ten you say *till all the streams gang dry, my dear*. My useful dictionary defines *gang* as a band of ruffians or criminals, a number of labourers working together. None of these definitions seem to fit."

I said that *gang* was also a Scottish transitive and intransitive verb meaning *go* and these words were a quotation from Robert Burns's greatest love song. My host murmured politely, "I believe Robert Burns's poetry is still sung in parts of North America."

I nodded. I was happy.

We were in the Smooth Groove, which had been the Central Station Hotel in days when Glasgow was joined to other places by railway. I felt the luxury of a good meal in my stomach, good wine on my palate, clean socks, underwear and shirt against my skin. They had been worth waiting for. Foreign translators, journalists and writers of dissertations always buy me new clothes before standing me a lunch – posh restaurants won't let me in without new clothes after I've slept a few weeks in ones the last foreigner bought me. But pubs and all-night cafés accept me since I learned to sleep in short snatches sitting upright. Foreigners contact me through my bank.

I was not always dependent on foreigners for a smart appearance. I used to have several friends with homes and visited each of them once a fortnight. They gave me food and a bed for the night and put my clothes through a machine. Modern machines not only wash, dry and iron, they remove stains, mend holes, replace lost buttons and redye faded fabric to look like new. Or am I dreaming that? If I am dreaming such a machine it is certainly possible because, as William Blake said, nothing exists which was not first dreamed. Most of these friends steadily disappeared but were not, I think, stabbed or burned. People with homes still usually die of diseases or a silly accident.

My one remaining friend is now my first wife who pretends to be my daughter. I don't know why. I visited her a month ago. After enjoying a plate of her excellent soup I asked how Mavis was getting on in London. She stared and said, "I am Mavis. Cathy is dead – died twelve years ago, shortly after I came home."

"Nonsense Cathy!" I said. "You can't be Mavis because Mavis quarrelled with you and she was right to quarrel with you because you were not kind to her, though I was too tactful to say so at the time."

My host was as ancient as I am and still used a note-book. Looking up from it he said, "I hear there is now no middle class in Scotland and England. Is that true?"

I told him it was not true: the middle class are those who used to be called working class – they have jobs but no investments, and their only pensions are state pensions.

"But middle class implies a lower class. Who are they?"

I explained that thieves, swindlers, rapists, drug deal-ers and murderers are our lower class nowadays, many of them registered with the police. They have a place in society because without them police, lawyers, judges, gaolers and journalists would be unemployed, and the profits of drug companies would slump.

"So in Britain everyone has a place in the social fabric?"

"Everyone but the homeless," I answered, trying to remember why I feel perfectly secure though I am one of these.

My host started writing again and to avoid disturbing thoughts I dreamed of a future state in which human police had disappeared because the rich no longer needed them. The rich never left their luxurious, well-defended homes except when visiting each other in vehicles mov-ing at the speed of light. Each home was protected by a metallic creature the size of a kitten and resembling a cockroach. It hid under chairs and sideboards and was programmed to kill intruders. I was a low-class criminal who broke into the apartment of a rich young sexy woman, cunningly reprogrammed her police creature to serve me, then enjoyed a number of sexual acts which appeared to be drawn in a highly coloured, very entertaining strip cartoon of a kind which became popular at the end of the twentieth century. Britain was a very entertaining country in those days. I had been teaching abroad since the late seventies and every time I returned the changes struck me as so interesting that I wrote about them. British people still read in those days.

Yes, one year publishers sold my stories to a newspaper cartoon supplement for so much that I stopped teaching and brought my second wife home to Glasgow. She was Californian or Chicagan, I think, and believed that life for prosperous people was the same anywhere, and indeed Britain was now very like America. The police only patrolled the streets of prosperous ghettos where householders had bought crime insurance. The police observed other communities through public surveillance cameras and had power to swoop in and lift up anyone on suspicion, but they mainly lifted unregistered politicians and folk who owed money to drug dealers. When people fell down in the street it was no longer etiquette to help them up or summon an ambulance. We hurried past knowing that next day they would probably be gone. I had a lovely home in those days. I lost it in a wave of inflation which suddenly made life *astonishingly* interesting. My wife returned to the USA. I stayed out of curiosity, though British publishing stopped. Industries with a use for wood and rag pulp bought the remaining libraries. Some books are still used to give public houses an old-fashioned look. Boys' adventure stories from the 1910s predominate.

My host said, "Toward the end of your eleventh book you mention *no concurrency of bone*. What do you mean by that?"

All foreigners ask that question. I can now answer it

without thinking. While doing so I closed my eyes and enjoyed walking on a grassy hilltop beside a tall, slender, beautiful young woman I had loved when I was fifty. Even in this dream I knew our love was in the past, that my virility was dead and that no beautiful woman would ever love me again. I told her this. She grew angry and called me selfish because I was only dreaming of her to cheer myself up. This was obviously true so I forgot her by staring at a hill on the far side of a valley, a Scottish hill soaring to Alpine heights with all the buildings I have ever known in rows between strips of woodland, heather and rocky cliffs. On the crest of the mountain I saw the red sandstone gable of the tenement where I was born in 1934, at the bottom the grey clocktower of the Smooth Groove where I was dining and dreaming. The scene delighted me by its blend of civilization and wilderness, by the ease with which the eye grasped so much rich intricacy. Suddenly the colour drained from it. The heather turned grey, the trees leafless, but I still felt perfectly safe and remembered why.

Though still telling my host about the massacre of Glencoe and Ezekiel's valley of dry bones I remembered the death of Mr Anderson, a former radio announcer with whom I once shared a kind of cave, a very safe secret little hidy-hole, we thought, in a shrubbery of Kelvingrove Park. In those days I had not learned to sleep in small snatches while sitting upright, I slept by drinking half a bottle of methylated spirits. One morning I woke to find my companion had been stabbed to death and scalped. I did not know why I had been spared until several weeks or months or years later. Perhaps it was yesterday. I'm sure I did not dream it.

I stood on the canal towpath enjoying a glorious gold, green and lavender sunset when I was tripped and knocked down. I lay flat on my back surrounded by children of seven, eight or nine. Their sex was not obvious. All wore black jeans and leather jackets. All had skulls and crossbones painted or tattooed on top of heads that were bald except for a finger of small pigtails all round. One poured petrol over my trousers, the rest waved bats, cutting implements, firelighters and discussed which part of me to bruise, cut or set fire to first.

"We are the death squad of the Maryhill Cleansing Brigade," explained the leader who was perhaps eleven or twelve. "We are licensed terrorists with a sacred mission to save the British economy through a course of geriatric disposal. Too many old gerries are depressing the economy these days. If you can't afford to get rejuvenated, grampa, you should have the decency to top yourself before becoming a burden to the state."

I told him I wasn't a burden to the state, wasn't even a beggar, that money was paid into my bank account by foreign publishers and was enough to feed me though not enough to rent a room.

"You pathetic, hairy old driveller!" shouted the leader, goading himself or herself into a fury. "You're an eye-sore! The visual equivalent of a force-nine-gale fart! You will die in hideous agony as a warning to others."

I was alarmed but excited. To die must be an awfully big adventure. Then a small fat person with glasses said, "Wait a bit Jimsy, I think he's famous."

They consulted a folded sheet with a lot of faces and names printed on it. The fat person, who could read names, asked if I was Mr Thingumajig, which I am. They helped me up, dusted me down, shook my hand very solemnly one at a time, said they would remember me next time we met, said they would gladly kill any old friend I wanted rid off, advised me not to go near a naked flame before my trousers were dry, hoped I had no hard feelings. Honestly, I had none at all. My gratitude and love for these children was so great that I wept real tears. The leader got me to autograph the printed sheet. It was pleasant to meet a young Scot who valued my signature. The sun had not yet set when they left me. I watched the gloaming fade, warm in the knowledge that I had a privileged place in modern Britain. Not only the children liked me but their bosses in the Cleansing Company or Social Security Trust or whoever has a use for children nowadays.

Yes, somebody up there likes me even though once I detested the bastards up there, the agents and consultants, money farmers and middle men, parliamentary quangomongers and local monopolists. My books were attacks on these people but caused no hard feelings, and now my books are only read in nations that lost World War Two.

My host spoke on a politely insistent note.

"I suggest you visit my country. Your royalties there will easily rent a private apartment with housekeeper and health care. We are no longer a military nation. We revere old people, which is why they live longer among us than anywhere else."

I said I was happy where I am. He shut his notebook and bowed saying, "You are a true master. You have subdued your wishes to your surroundings."

This angered me but I did not show it. There are better ways of living than being happy but they require strength and sanity. The weak are as incapable of sanity as the rich. In this country sanity would drive the weak to suicide and make the rich distinctly uncomfortable. We are better without it.